SM

5/. 4/39

AT HOME IN THE FIELDS

BLACKIE & SON LIMITED
50 Old Bailey, LONDON
17 Stanhope Street, GLASGOW

BLACKIE & SON (INDIA) LIMITED
Warwick House, Fort Street, BOMBAY

BLACKIE & SON (CANADA) LIMITED
TORONTO

AT HOME
IN THE FIELDS

BY

B. MELVILLE NICHOLAS

BLACKIE & SON LIMITED
LONDON AND GLASGOW

In the Same Series:

  AT HOME IN THE WOODS.
  AT HOME ABOUT HEDGEROWS
    AND HOMESTEADS.

First published 1938

Printed in Great Britain by Blackie & Son, Ltd., Glasgow

CONTENTS

LIST OF PLATES

vii

LIST OF PLATES

THE RABBIT

IF rabbits were less common we should appreciate them more, but because of their numbers they have become a nuisance and a menace, and every man's hand is against them.

Yet, although now so amazingly abundant, the rabbit was not always a denizen of Britain. Just when it was first introduced is difficult to tell, but records would seem to give the credit for the animal's introduction here to the Normans when they first settled in this country.

During those early years rabbits were greatly prized and strictly protected; rabbit meat was regarded as a luxury, and even when the animals had become fairly abundant, their popularity did not lessen until comparatively recent times. During the last few years, however, there can be no doubt that the rabbit has become a serious pest to agriculture. Many millions of pounds worth of crops are destroyed by rabbits annually in this country, and there is little wonder why the subject of keeping in check the rabbit population has received of late so much publicity. Even Government committees have devoted much

1

attention to this little brown animal of our fields, but, in spite of all that has been said, done or hoped for, the rabbit continues to flourish and increase.

During the past spring and summer (1937) I have made exhaustive inquiries concerning rabbits, and have found that in most districts they are more numerous than ever before. I think this may be explained by two reasons: firstly, that as the winter of 1936 was a particularly mild one, rabbits continued to breed almost throughout the whole winter. In November of that year I unearthed a litter of rabbits about ten days old, while, in nearby fields, youngsters were to be seen at Christmas taking their first excursions. Not far from my home in Cornwall is a field through which runs a stream. On the banks of this stream primroses grow in great profusion, and are usually in bloom by the middle of January. I gathered my first primroses there last winter on January the sixteenth, and on that day a mother rabbit and her four children—the latter no more than three weeks old—were seen on the primrose-decked bank, enjoying a brief interval of winter sunshine.

I sometimes wonder whether rabbits are able to appreciate beauty, for I know of a family that has come to reside amid snowdrops that grow close to a brook, and other instances of rabbits

2

making their homes in congenial and beautiful surroundings have often come to my notice. A friend of mine recently planted some rhododendrons in a small coppice which he intends to set aside as a bird sanctuary. No sooner did the shrubs bloom than a rabbit excavated its residence among the roots. It was a pretty sight to watch this rabbit come forth to its evening meal, pause a few seconds at the entrance to its home to perform a toilet, then leave the shelter of its rhododendron home for the grassy plots ahead.

Few British animals are more interesting than rabbits, or have more commendable ways. No creature takes more trouble to keep clean and tidy. A dirty rabbit is a most unusual spectacle, which, considering that it lives most of its life underground, is rather remarkable. Watch a rabbit come out to feed, and almost without exception it will pause on the threshold of its home, as did the rabbit under the rhododendron shrubs, to clean itself, and shake the soil from its paws before proceeding to its pastures.

In common with most animals rabbits dislike wet herbage, and may often be seen shaking the water from their paws when crossing fields. A heavy rainfall often makes matters very uncomfortable for them, for not only does it make the surface wet, but often results in the flooding of their subterranean homes. Under such circumstances, the refugees find shelter in residences above ground-level, sometimes having to take cover on the ground itself, concealing themselves as best they can in a hedgerow or amid herbage, or bracken.

The rabbit's sole means of progression is by hopping—it never walks or runs. It is able to travel very quickly and, on such occasions, the hind feet come past the fore feet. When it is running from danger nothing is more obvious than the white underparts of the rabbit's tail. It is only when alarmed that the tail is held aloft, and there has been much conjecture as to the purpose of this white tail, or " scut ", as it is called. The most popular theory is that the tail acts as a danger signal to other rabbits in the same pastures, and although one may at first be inclined to ridicule this idea there are one or two points which would tend to support it. Firstly, we have to remember that it is only when suspicious, or in danger, that the animal exhibits its white tail; the scut is not visible when the rabbit is feeding, or leisurely hopping about, which would seem to suggest that the white tail is a danger, or warning signal; secondly, when we consider the gregarious habits of rabbits, we readily see the immense value of such a signal. Such a token would not, of course, be of the slightest use to the solitary hare, and, consequently, we do not find it displayed on this animal. Against this theory, however, it has been argued that whilst the bobbing white tail of the escaping rabbit may be a useful warning to other rabbits, it is an increased danger to that particular rabbit itself. I have read somewhere of a boy, who, in reply to a question on a general knowledge paper asking: " Why has a rabbit a white tail?", replied, " To provide a mark to shoot at."

If a rabbit fancies danger, it stamps on the ground with its hind feet. The sound thus made carries a considerable distance and gives warning to other rabbits in the vicinity to be on the alert. It is then most interesting to watch them sit up on their hind legs, listening for whatever signs the breeze may bring them. If there is any sign of danger, they at once bolt to cover, the bobbing white tails of the older animals showing the younger and less experienced ones in which direction to run for safety.

I am inclined to believe that, in the majority of rabbit cities, sentinels are appointed, just as in every rookery certain rooks are appointed to keep guard. In a particular meadow which I have long kept under observation rabbits are very numerous; in fact, they are never trapped or disturbed, for the old fellow who owns the land enjoys the company of " the happy, playful bunnies ", as he calls them. It was only after considerable persuasion that I was permitted to enter the meadow for the purpose of photographing a young cuckoo, although in an adjoining field I had often watched and photographed the rabbits. In the meadow in question it looked as if the rabbit population would be faced with insufficient food, for the grass was getting rather scanty and, realizing this, the old fellow—well over seventy years of age— would bring them lettuce, cabbages and carrots. If I had not seen with my own eyes I would never have believed the friendliness and understanding which existed between him and his rabbit guests. The rabbits would follow him about the meadow just like cats or dogs, and showed no fear whatever of his approach.

The majority of times when I watched that rabbit colony, the first rabbit to appear emerged from a ground hole on the eastern side of the meadow; the second rabbit would come forth from a hole on the western side—almost exactly opposite the home of the first rabbit. Both were fairly old rabbits, well used to the sounds and signs of the countryside, and they would sit listening for a few seconds, looking left and right in thoughtful uncertainty before leaving their thresholds. After a few moments had passed the other inhabitants would come out, until the meadow seemed literally alive with them. Whether the two rabbits which, almost invariably, appeared first were the town

6

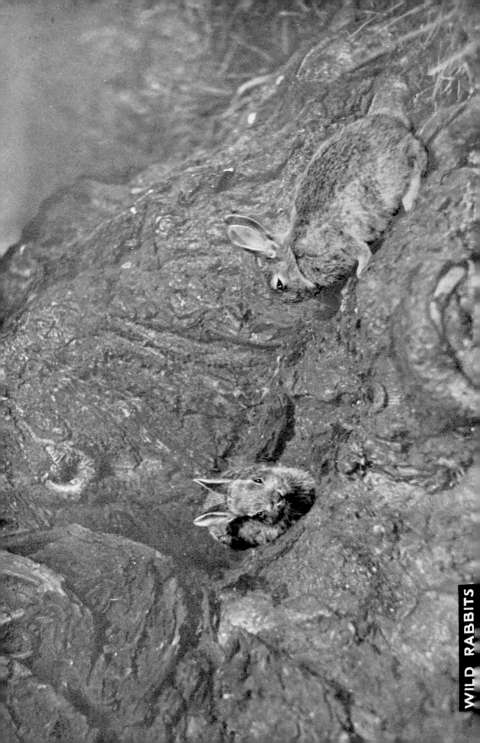

sentinels, I do not know, but once, when a dog strayed into the meadow, they were among the first to show the " white flag " of danger and warn the others to safety. Similar instances have led me to believe that there is an understanding of some sort among rabbits akin to the sentinel-ship of the rookery.

Rabbits prefer to make their own excavations, and if they are left undisturbed by other animals, such as foxes and badgers, their burrows often reach enormous proportions. Corridors and passage-ways are excavated, and side tunnels made until the ground, hedge or bank, as the case may be, becomes honey-combed through the activities of the inhabitants.

These burrows often provide a shelter for other animals, such as, for instance, the hedgehog, which may feel disposed to make its nest of leaves, moss and grass within the shelter of the burrow and, when the chilly winds of autumn begin to blow, " turn in " to sleep until the following spring. Sometimes squirrels, especially grey squirrels, take cover in rabbits' burrows, and rats are frequent visitors. Stoats and weasels are never welcome guests to a rabbit city, for they seldom come except on some bloodthirsty mission. I have found little owls, pheasants, and wheatears nesting in rabbit burrows, and on one occasion I discovered a nest of young song-thrushes in a side hole of a rabbit's den, whilst rabbits daily passed up and down the main entrance less than a foot from the feathered family. Of course, the song-thrush often does the most unexpected things, and is a close rival to the robin redbreast and the blue tit in its choice of queer nesting sites. Foxes often take possession of rabbit holes, slightly enlarging them to suit their convenience, finding it much easier to enlarge a rabbit burrow than to excavate a fresh home for themselves. Occasionally, a badger may do likewise, but it is a more rare usurper than the fox, as the badger prefers to dig its own fortress, which, with its strong legs and stiff, horny claws, it is able to accomplish with ease.

Although foxes and badgers are the enemies of rabbits, it is not unusual to find them living together in the same burrow, and in another book [1] I have referred to the rather strange behaviour of foxes and badgers when living in the same vicinity as rabbits, choosing to go farther afield to hunt rather than catch the rabbits that live in the same burrow.

The arch-enemy of the rabbit is, undoubtedly, the stoat, and the pitiful scream of a rabbit when being tracked by this bloodthirsty little bandit of the hedgerow is one of the most heart-rending sounds of the countryside. Yet if the sounds of

[1] *At Home in the Woods.*

the hunted rabbit are heart-rending, the *sight* of the bewildered and doomed-to-death little animal is really worse.

The most extraordinary thing about the stoat's attack is that it seems to rob the rabbit of all its swiftness of foot, and the fastest speed of which it is capable when being chased is but a slow, stumbling pace, until eventually, as the stoat approaches, the rabbit even loses the power of movement altogether and crouches squealing to await its deadly enemy. Naturalists differ in their explanation of the rabbit's behaviour, but it seems quite certain to me that the hunted animal is overcome by some sort of paralysis which affects its brain so that its limbs neglect to function. I have often rescued rabbits from the grip of stoats, when, except for a small wound where the stoat had fixed its grip, they have been none the worse for their experience. But the strangest thing of all happens when the rabbits are released, for, instead of scurrying off to cover, as one would expect them to, they stupidly hop about in circles and turn somersaults. This fact also supports my theory that the rabbit when being tracked by a stoat suffers from an affection of the brain, so that it ceases to be a normal or responsible animal. Whether to call it hypnotism or paralysis is an open question, but certain it is that the terrified rabbit becomes bereft of whatever reason it possessed, and does the most un-usual things. I well remember walking down a country lane at the back of my home in Cornwall in the early hours of a winter's morning, accom-panied by Rex, my Alsatian, when quite suddenly a rabbit came towards us. It was easy to see that the rabbit was being pursued, for its pace was neither the playful, care-free canter of the happy bunny nor the wild gallop of the normal chased rabbit. Instead, it ambled through the under-growth along by the hedgerow and finally stopped when only a few inches from my feet. I somehow doubt if the rabbit were conscious of my presence until I took it up. A few fields farther on I released it, when it acted in the same strange way referred to, which proves that whatever overcomes the rabbit is the outcome of fear rather than the direct result of the wound inflicted by the stoat.

Dogs, cats, foxes, badgers, owls and other birds of prey, are all the foes of the rabbit, but over and above the thousands of rabbits killed by these natural enemies, man is responsible for many more deaths. I have on many occasions voiced my disapproval, both in speech and in writing, of the terrible suffering inflicted on the rabbit population by the continued use of those cruel, steel-toothed gins, and this book is not, perhaps, a fit medium for debating the humani-tarian aspect of such a question, but it does seem a wicked and wanton shame to inflict hours and hours of torture on innocent rabbits when equally effective and far less cruel means of keeping down their numbers are available.

I do not write under the delusion that rabbits need not be trapped; quite the contrary, for every day of my life I see the damage they occasion to growing crops, but *must* they be killed by such a barbarous method? I have high hopes that the near future and the rising generation of animal lovers will definitely answer the question in the negative.

The rabbit is amazingly prolific, and the age at which it starts to breed would seem to vary, but I have known many instances where litters have been born to females three months old. Some litters, however, take longer to mature, and weather conditions greatly affect the domestic activities of rabbits. The normal breeding season for adults is from February to October, although, as I have already mentioned, under favourable weather conditions breeding often goes on all the year round. The real high-tide of domestic affairs in the rabbit warren is reached in May or June, when the fields and hedges teem with baby rabbits.

Litters born in summer may consist of as many as seven or eight, but earlier and later litters are smaller—two or three young are usual during late autumn or winter. Even so, it may be · realized that in the course of a few months the rabbit population of any warren or colony can increase to an alarming extent.

The family life of the rabbit is most interesting and, contrary to what is often believed, the young are seldom born in the burrow, but in a special hole, known as a " stop ", which the mother prepares herself. This hole or "stop " is seldom more than two feet deep and has but one entrance; at the end of the passage-way the female scrapes out a chamber, in which she afterwards makes a nest of dry grasses, lining it with fur scratched from her own body. In this cosy nursery the youngsters are born, naked and blind at first, and absolutely dependent upon their mother. The male rabbit takes no interest whatever in the offspring, for the probability is that he has several wives, and as he could not be equally attentive to all, he decides to treat them all alike and take no interest in any.

It is the mother alone to whom the credit is due for the rearing of the family. In her method of motherhood, however, she is quite unique among British animals in that she never remains with her young except when she returns during the night to feed them. All day long the young are left alone in the nursery, the mother taking care when leaving home to seal over the entrance with grass or fur, over which she scratches some soil.

When about twelve days old the eyes of the baby rabbits open, and in a few more days they take their first venture abroad. For a week or two they remain about the nursery under the careful guardianship of their mother, who is very brave in defence of her little ones. Foxes and badgers take toll of many young rabbits in their babyhood days, for with their keen scent Reynard and Brock are adept at finding these newly-born youngsters. It has been suggested by some writers, with, I think, a great deal of truth, that the reason why the mother rabbit never lies with her young is to avoid the risk of enemies scenting her presence.

When about a month or five weeks old the youngsters are taken by their mother into the main warren, where they either join in the communal life of their neighbours or return to their nursery and enlarge their old home to suit their needs. It often happens that a nursery forms the nucleus of a future warren, for the mother rabbit never uses the same " stop " for two families.

Sometimes a less energetic female decides to make a nursery in some quiet part of the main burrow, selecting more often than not a blind alley or side corridor, in which to bring forth her young, but the family seldom survives. The adult inhabitants of the warren seem to disapprove, refusing to allow the mother to return to feed her young, so that they die of starvation, or else they pull the nursery to pieces and scatter to left and right the young treasures.

Occasionally a female rabbit decides to choose an unusual site for her nursery. I recently found a litter of rabbits in an old hat that had blown off a scarecrow into the hedgerow. Firmly embedded among bracken and herbage which had grown up around it, the hat contained a family of five baby rabbits closely huddled together in a warm nest of fur.

Mr. H. S. Vickers of Immingham tells me of a rabbit that made her nursery and reared her family of eight on the quay at Immingham Dock. Mr. Vickers writes: " Trains of timber were actually shunting over these lines, for the nest itself was made in a mere scrape, just under the rail and almost in the centre of the quay which, just then, was a hive of industry. The mother stayed under an adjacent pile of timber during the day, returning to her young at night."

Out of the hundreds of acres of grass land adjoining the Dock Estate at Immingham, it seems strange that this rabbit should have chosen such an unusual and busy place for her nursery.

Although wild rabbits confine their activities chiefly to early morning and evenings, they often

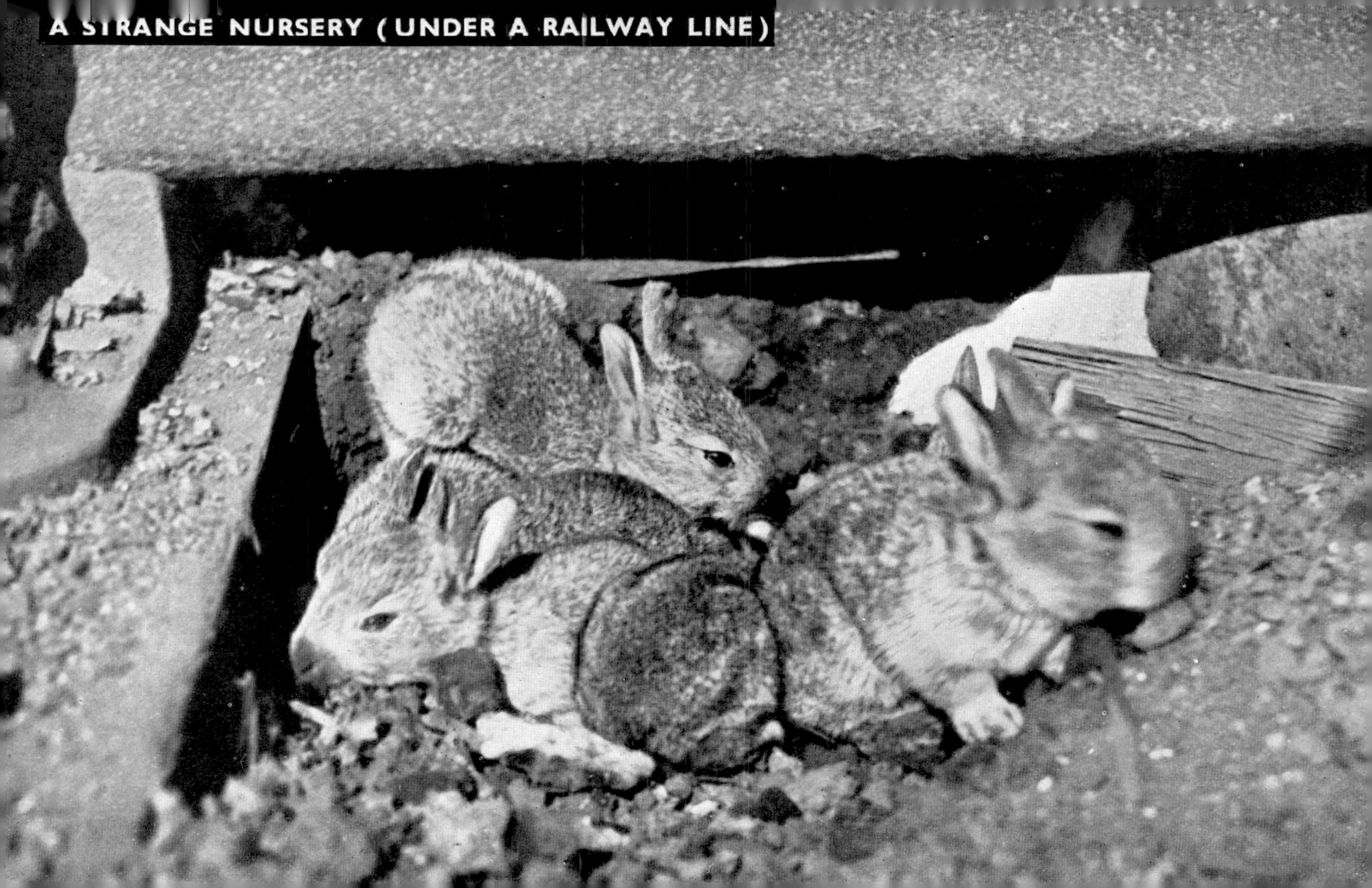

A STRANGE NURSERY (UNDER A RAILWAY LINE)

"BUNNY" AT HIS FRONT DOOR

come abroad at all hours of the day and night.
In districts where they are not disturbed they
frequently spend hours basking in the sunshine.
They are defenceless creatures and rely solely on
speed to save their lives in the presence of danger.
They possess, however, a remarkable instinct to
conceal themselves well amid herbage or bracken,
and thus evade their enemies.

The rabbit gives an example of the danger of
introducing an animal into a country foreign to
it, for the introduction of the rabbit into Australia
—where the climatic conditions proved especially
suitable to its prolificacy—has had very serious
consequences.

It is estimated that over 1,000,000,000 rabbits
are destroyed annually in Australia, yet their
numbers seem to increase, with the result that
hundreds of acres of crops are destroyed each year.

If taken young, rabbits make ideal pets, and
soon give their friendship and confidence in
return for food and shelter. Yet individual
specimens vary in their temperament, and it is
more or less a gamble as to how they will react
to human advances. During the last ten years I
have kept several wild rabbits, some of them
making delightful pets, whilst others have never
lost their natural fear and suspicion.

" Sheen ", which I found when she was but a
wee creature crossing a woodland path, readily

took to domestic surroundings, and never once showed any inclination to roam. Eventually, when given the freedom of a large garden, she still preferred not to stray, and lived for three years as a household pet. Normally Sheen was good tempered, but she never seemed agreeable towards Jock, an Alsatian, which shared her private territory; the two animals often had differences, quarrelled and parted; but I never thought any serious outcome would result for they were reared together, and Jock would instantly protect Sheen from any trespassing canine or feline creatures. One evening, however, a scuffle was heard in the garden and the dead body of Sheen was afterwards discovered under a rose bush. Exactly what the dispute was about no one will ever know, but the look in Jock's eyes told plainly that he was the murderer.

THE HOMELESS HARES

IN outward appearance the brown hare closely resembles the rabbit, except that the hare is bigger, with longer ears and legs. Like the rabbit it depends upon its swiftness for safety; it is able to travel at an amazing speed, and to keep up its pace for an incredibly long time. It is a homeless animal, having no burrow to resort to for refuge and, when chased, has to outrun its pursuer, or die.

Hares prefer the flat, open country, and owing to the fact that their hind limbs are nearly twice as long as their fore limbs, they are better able to travel uphill than down. They are also able to "double back" at a very sharp angle (a trait also noticeable in the fox) without slackening their speed, and this has often been their salvation; many a dog has indulged in a few somersaults before being able to reverse its course, thus giving the hare an opportunity to put many yards of ground between it and its pursuer.

When running the hind feet strike the ground ahead of the fore feet, and the animal is more concerned with things behind than with what may

17

be ahead, with the result that it has often collided with people and animals in its eagerness to escape its pursuers. The prominent eyes of the hare are so situated as to enable the animal to see backwards almost as easily as forwards without turning its head.

Although, as I have already stated, superficially resembling the rabbit, the hare differs from its smaller relatives in its habits and home-life. These differences are nowhere more noticeable than in the nursery, for whereas baby rabbits are born blind and helpless in a cosy nest, baby hares —or leverets as they are called—are clothed in a coat of soft fur and born with their eyes wide open. For a few days, however, they are helpless little creatures, and it is a mystery how so many of them survive, for they have no warm, concealed nursery such as the mother rabbit prepares for her family. Hares are homeless animals, all their lives being lived above ground. Their resting places are known as " forms ", and are merely flattened out chambers amid growing herbage, with a few growing stalks or grass stems to shelter and conceal them. It is in a nursery such as this that the female hare brings forth her young, being two, three or four, and sometimes five in number. The pairing and breeding season is from March to September, but in mild seasons breeding may go on all the year round. It is in March, particularly, that the males seem to take domestic matters seriously, and engage in all sorts of frolic and play in order to win as many fair ladies as possible. There is much jumping, running and excitement among these " Jack " hares, as sportsmen often call the males, which has probably given rise to the familiar expression " as mad as a March hare ". Not infrequently fights occur between two males which covet the same spouse, but it is rare that serious injury results to either of the combatants.

In common with rabbits, the males take no interest in the rearing of their young, and leave the offspring entirely to the care of the mother, but she, on the other hand, is a most devoted parent, brave in defence of her little ones and sparing herself no trouble to supply their every need. Not being equipped with powerful weapons to wage a warfare to protect her family, the mother hare has to do the best she can by kicking with her hind legs, and many and hard are the knocks she is able to deliver in this way. Many a stoat has had to retreat from its bloodthirsty purpose as a result of the mother hare's retaliation in the way mentioned, and not infrequently grazing horses, cows and sheep receive severe blows for trespassing, quite unconsciously, of course, near a hare's nursery.

The leverets do not stay in the nursery long,

but scatter and make fresh forms of their own. Seldom, if ever, do the whole litter settle in the same form, but instead they separate in two or more parties, each party having its own form. I believe the mother hare plays an important part in the separation of her family and assists them in the selection of suitable sites. Certain it is that she visits each form regularly, and if she finds that either party has been discovered she at once removes them to safer quarters.

The mother hare emits a harsh cry when calling her young, the latter replying with a sharp, shrill squeak. This is in striking contrast to rabbits, which are silent animals except when in danger or when suffering.

Leverets, when resting or in their forms, are most difficult to find, as their brown-and-grey fur so perfectly matches the colouring of their surroundings as to produce an excellent example of protective coloration. They also have the instinct to remain motionless until an intruder is perilously near. This is also a habit of the adult hare, which seems to be able to realize at once when it has been discovered. Unless the squatting hare knows that it has been seen (how it is able to know is a mystery), it remains in its form even though one may be within a few inches of it. I am inclined to believe that a suspicious hare watches the gaze rather than the position of an intruder, and the

20

moment it realizes that it has been seen it runs
for its very life's sake.

Leverets, however, are not able to escape with
such speed, but being smaller are endowed with
excellent powers of concealment and are able to
disappear under one's very eyes. The instinct to
hide is an essential part of a hare's life, for it
must be remembered that the animal has no
underground retreat or other refuge to which to
escape, and the only protection it has is the insecure
shelter or concealment it can find behind grass or
herbage. Of all British animals the hare is the
most homeless and defenceless. Many a hare
owes its life to its protective coloration.

The common hare is normally of a brownish-
grey colour, with white under parts, but occasionally black specimens are seen, and even white
hares have been recorded.

The animal has remarkably acute hearing, and
the question is often debated as to whether a hare
ever closes its eyes. It is almost impossible to find
a wild hare asleep, but from my experience of
domesticated hares, I can definitely state that a
hare *does* close its eyes. One tame hare in particular which I became acquainted with would
close its eyes and doze while being fondled. It is
different, however, with hares at large, for I have
never been able to find a wild hare asleep, or
even off its guard. No doubt the softest footfall

or tremor of the earth is felt by the squatting animal.

The hare, like the rabbit, never walks, but progresses by short hops, or leaps, and, under pressure, is able to cover a distance of nine or ten feet at one leap. It is also able to maintain this speed for long distances, although, normally, a hare does not, in the early stages of a chase, gallop at its fastest speed. If it can keep a safe distance ahead of the pursuing hounds it is satisfied, preferring to keep a reserve of strength to tire out its enemies in a long run. Hares usually know the land for miles around their dwelling-places, and will, when possible, make for the open country, leading the hounds uphill where, as we have already seen, the hare can, owing to its longer hind limbs, make more speed.

Hounds hunt by scent, and the hare's first duty, after having gained a reasonable distance over its pursuers, is to put the hounds off the scent. Several ruses have been employed by hares in order to accomplish this, but none more frequent than that of crossing a stream. I do not think hares take to water except under pressure, as they are not good swimmers. When floating, the animal's back is lower than its hind parts, the latter being raised well above the surface of the water.

A hare has wonderful leaping powers, and will

leap clean over gates or hedges. It will leap five or six feet vertically into the air from a squatting posture, which, more often than not, is their method of leaving their form when disturbed.

Normally hares are solitary creatures, spending the hours of daylight in their forms, usually situated on elevated ground, with as much protection as possible both from the weather and from observation. In the evening, when they come forth to feed, they do so with great caution, and it is seldom that more than one animal is seen on the same feeding-ground. Exceptions, of course, do occur, and I have seen four hares feeding within an area of ten square yards. In early spring the animals associate preparatory for the breeding season.

The food, like that of rabbits, is vegetarian, and hares often travel many miles in order to feed from some favourite food. Young cabbages are a favourite delicacy, and a distance of a few miles is nothing to a hare if a good meal is the reward for the journey. Yet the animal will take advantage of a short cut to a favourite feeding-ground, and an instance bearing out this statement recently came under my observation. A stream, some twelve or thirteen feet across, divided a patch of cabbages from a hare's dwelling-place, and as it was discovered that a hare regularly visited the cabbage patch, it was wondered whether the

animal swam the stream or travelled by foot—
a distance of some two miles. To decide the point
a watch was kept, when it was discovered that the
hare adopted neither of the two methods suggested; instead, the wily animal utilized a fallen
tree that spanned the stream, cautiously hopping
over the trunk to the cabbage patch and back
again.

The brown hare is generally distributed over
England and Wales, and also in certain parts of
Scotland, but in the higher mountainous districts
its place is taken by the blue, or mountain, hare.

The blue, or mountain, hare is smaller than
the brown one of the English countryside, and
has shorter ears. The name " blue " hare is
really a misnomer, for at no time is the fur of the
animal actually blue. The general colour is a
tawny-grey, with greyish-white under sides; the
ears are tipped with black as are the ears of our
brown hares. The fur is softer and thicker than
that of the brown hare, and in winter the mountain hare changes colour, assuming a coat of pure
white, except for its black ear-tips. As would be
expected, the change of coat takes place gradually,
and in some specimens sooner than in others.
In autumn it is quite a common spectacle to see
mountain hares wearing pure white coats, while
other hares have scarcely begun to shed their
summer pelage; others may be half through the

change, being a patch-work of grey, white and brown. Normally the moult takes place between September and November, although later and earlier changes in the animals' pelage occurs. One certainty about this change of pelage is that the hare never loses the black tips to its ears.

The mountain hare and the stoat are the only two British animals that undergo an annual change of coat, and even so it is only those stoats inhabiting northern regions that do so. In the cases of both animals there is a similarity, in that, whilst the hare retains its black-tipped ears, the stoat's black-tipped tail never alters.

The change back to summer pelage is usually complete by the early days of May, and, like the autumnal change, is a gradual process, although there seems to be more uniformity in the actual moult.

Although natives of Scotland and some of the islands, mountain hares have been introduced into some northern counties of England and into Wales, where, in certain districts, they have established themselves.

The animal is not capable of such speed as the brown hare, which is, perhaps, to be expected when one considers the type of country which it inhabits. In its mountainous districts, however, it has a distinct advantage over the brown hare of the fields and lowlands in that it is able to take refuge among rocks and boulders. It is surprising into what a small crevice a hunted mountain hare will push itself, but the smaller the refuge the greater the animal's safety, for its pursuer is usually the bigger of the two.

The mountain hare is really more nomadic in its behaviour than its brown cousin, for whilst the latter has its own form, which it calls " home ", the mountain hare seldom has any such recognized residence. Crevices in rocks and among boulders are the mountain hare's resting places, but the average animal does not acknowledge one particular place more than another as its own abode. The animal is a born wanderer, and if no rocks are available when it feels tired or in need of a rest, it merely settles down among growing heather or tall grasses to await the twilight or until danger drives it forth into the open again.

In its domestic habits it closely resembles the brown hare in that the young are born clothed in fur and with their prominent eyes wide open. The nursery is an exposed situation among rocky crags or in growing vegetation, where the leverets are exposed to the often cold and unpleasant weather of the mountains.

When old enough the leverets scatter into independent forms in companies of twos or threes. Whether this separation of the family is the result of the instinct of the leverets themselves, or carried out by the mother, is a point that is often debated, just as it is in relation to the brown hare. Owing to the animal's activities being confined to the twilight, and also owing to their being such wary and suspicious creatures, observation is rendered difficult. The general consensus of opinion is to the effect that the work is carried out by the thoughtful mother, but some naturalists argue otherwise, on the grounds that such a course would tend to make the care and upbringing of her family all the more difficult for her. There is, naturally, a certain amount of reason behind that suggestion, for it undoubtedly does entail more work to visit three or four forms than to visit one, but in support of the theory that it is the mother's desire that her family separate, is the fact that hares have many enemies — foxes, badgers, weasels, dogs, cats, and so forth, and if any such predatory creatures discover the nursery tragedy overtakes all the inhabitants. How much safer, therefore, to have the family in different forms, so that, even though one form be discovered, the others may escape detection. This has happened on many occasions, and the fact that the different forms are often a dozen, or even twenty yards apart, seems to support this theory.

Three or four litters are produced in a year, and the number to a litter may be anything from

27

two to eight. Other names for the mountain, or blue hare, are the Alpine and variable hare.

The Irish hare, which is indigenous to Ireland, is brown in general colour, except in winter, when there is a partial change in the animal's coat. It never becomes perfectly white, however, and there are always prominent patches of brown, especially about the forehead and flanks. In common with other hares, it retains its black-tipped ears. In size, it is smaller than the brown hare and considerably larger than the mountain hare, and is common all over Ireland. It has been introduced into various parts of England, Wales and Scotland.

The domestic habits of the Irish hare are similar to those of the brown and the mountain hares. Three, four, and sometimes five, litters are produced in a year, the young being brought forth without even the scantiest of preparations. A cleft or crevice among rocks is the usual nursery, but occasionally a form in heather or bracken is made.

BROWN HARE

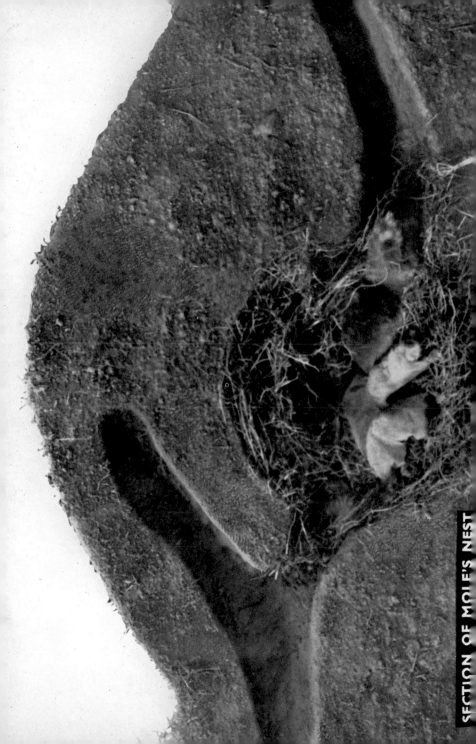

SECTION OF MOLE'S NEST

THE MOLE

BETWEEN the homeless hare, whose life is lived above ground, and the mole, whose whole existence, with rare exceptions, is spent underground, is as great a contrast as can be found between any two British mammals.

How very different must be the life of the hare, with its keen, wide-open eyes, as it views the glories of the countryside, to the life of the mole in its subterranean tunnels, where it is unable to see anything.

The mole, or " the little gentleman in the black velvet coat", as it is often called, has eyes, but they are so tiny—no bigger than pin-pricks— and so deeply buried in the animal's fur that they are of no use. I believe it can distinguish daylight from darkness, but that is all; and even if it could see, its eyes would be of very little use in the dark underground tunnels in which it lives.

Because of its habits of living underground, the mole is a most difficult animal to study. It seldom shows itself on the surface, and, even when it does emerge through the soil into view, it just as suddenly disappears again.

Yet, although so seldom seen, its presence is made known by the hillocks of soil, or " mole-hills " as they are called, which the animal throws up when making its underground thoroughfares.

For its size the mole is probably the strongest British mammal. It burrows its way through the ground with remarkable ease, and a tunnel of fifty yards in length is often a mole's day's work. Naturally it prefers damp soil, because digging is easier, but there is another reason, for the mole is very fond of earth worms, and needs plenty of water.

The hillocks of earth thrown up by moles vary in size, the average being about ten inches or a foot in height, and about eighteen inches in diameter. Larger ones are quite common, and in cultivated areas it is easy to realize the damage moles can do to growing crops.

Mole-hills are the living apartments of moles, for about a foot below ground is a chamber about the size of a small football, which is the mole's home. Here a warm, cosy nest of grasses and moss is made, in which the little animal spends whatever time it can spare. Being the busy, industrious creature it is, however, it rests but very seldom, for daylight and darkness are all the same to the mole.

It is active both day and night, and digging is accomplished at a great speed. Most of the digging is done with the animal's fore paws, these being exceptionally broad, with five toes to each paw, and set laterally to the body. The four feet of the mole are short and strong, pinkish in colour, and each toe is fitted with a sharp claw.

Although the mole is seldom seen above ground, it is evident that it does visit the surface to collect materials for its nest. This is probably done in the darkness, otherwise the animal would most certainly have been more often observed at work. To gather these materials must be a great effort for the mole, and I have always noticed that its nest is composed of the materials most easily available.

In making its underground residence and highways the mole excavates its nest chamber first, the displaced earth becoming the familiar mole-hill. A number of tunnels are then excavated, some leading from the chamber to above ground, whilst others are of a zigzag course, crossing and recrossing each other with numerous culs-de-sac along the route.

Old natural history books would lead us to believe that moles follow a recognized system in their tunnelling, and whilst my own observations prove the similarity in the actual tunnels themselves, I have found nothing to suggest any uniformity of arrangement in these mole thoroughfares. A great deal of skill is displayed in all mole excavations, but I think each animal follows its own individual instinct, and just burrows its way here, there and anywhere, according to its desires.

The presence of these culs-de-sac to which I have already referred has been the subject of much divergence of opinion, but it seems probable that they are used by one mole to step aside to allow another mole, travelling in the opposite direction, to proceed. Similar culs-de-sac are present in the runs of field mice and voles, especially those of the short-tailed field vole, and I have no doubt but that their object in all cases is the same. Two moles could not pass each other in the same run, and it is a well-known fact that several moles use the same thoroughfares; therefore the theory I have put forth seems to be a likely one.

It is often easy to trace a mole run by the arching of the soil caused by the run being so near to the surface. Sometimes these runs are made from hillock to hillock, but at other times they proceed in a zigzag course for several yards without communicating with any mole-hills. In light soil it is often possible to detect the where-abouts of a mole as it moves along its tunnel, and occasionally one is privileged to see a little pink nose push its way out of the soil quickly to be drawn back again.

Although different moles traverse the same highway, there is nothing of the gregarious spirit among the animals. The fact that a number occupy the same territory is because of the food available there, and not because any friendliness exists among them. Worms, insects, grubs, snails, slugs, and such like, are the mainstay of moles, and they have voracious appetites. Water is a most essential item for them, and it is not surprising, therefore, that they usually take up residence within the vicinity of running water. Quite often their surface runs lead to water, and the mole is quite a good swimmer.

The animal's fur coat has no particular " set " one way or another, and it can just as easily travel along its tunnels backwards as forwards. The velvety blue-black fur, therefore, does not easily become soiled or displaced, and no matter whether you stroke it backwards or forwards, it still remains smooth.

In fact it would be difficult to find a more classic example of adaptation to environment, and for a mole to live under any other circumstances than those of its natural underground surroundings would be impossible.

Naturally, because of its structural build for work underground, one would not expect a mole to be capable of any great speed when running over the surface, but this is a mistake, and when travelling on ground for leisure or hunting, a mole proceeds very quickly. On the other hand, a mole seldom runs any distance

when liberated or if it knows it is being watched
—under such conditions, it goes to earth at
once. I have often liberated moles just to see how
quickly and easily they disappear into the ground
—in a few seconds they vanish into the earth.
A mole, if it gets the chance, will bite, but although
it might bring the blood, I have never known any
real or lasting harm result. The animal's most
formidable weapons are its sharp toe-nails, and
these it can use to good purpose in its own
defence.

Moles fight a great deal among themselves,
especially during the mating season, when it would
seem that the females are the worst offenders.
Battles commenced underground are often finished
on the surface, the stronger combatant chasing
the weaker into the open, where the dispute
sometimes ends fatally. Dead moles on the surface
are by no means unusual, and I am inclined to
believe that many of them die quite suddenly
from natural causes. I have also found dead bodies
in their nests, with no sign of violence to explain
the tragedy.

The mole has no external ears, but its sensitive
body records every footfall and tremor of the
earth, so that the animal probably " hears "
better without ears than most animals can with
them. The sense of smell and touch are also
very acute, and it is upon these that the mole

largely relies when finding its way about and when hunting.

The breeding nest of the female mole is smaller than that of its normal residence, with a correspondingly smaller hillock, and some writers declare that the female is alone responsible for the making of these nurseries. Whether or not that is so I cannot say, but I do not think the sexes associate except during the mating season.

The young are born in May, and at birth are naked and flesh-coloured, but the skin gradually darkens, and when about three weeks old a coating of fur is present. Another two or three weeks see the youngsters able to forage for themselves, but the parents rear only one litter each year.

Four or five young are the usual number for one litter, but eight have been recorded.

The mole is widely distributed throughout England, Wales and Scotland, and although the normal colour is bluish-black, whitish-grey specimens sometimes occur. It is not present in Ireland.

According to history, William of Orange met his death through the horse which he was riding stepping on a mole-hill. The Jacobites afterwards used to drink to the health of the " little gentleman in the black velvet coat ", a title which the mole fraternity has retained to the present day.

THE HARVEST MOUSE

THE harvest mouse is a small and fragile little creature, sandy-red in colour, with whitish under parts, there being a clearly defined line of demarcation. The nose and feet are flesh colour, and, but for the pygmy shrew, it would have the distinction of being the smallest British mammal.

Although scarcely bigger than the top of one's thumb, this little animal is quite an accomplished acrobat, able to run up and down corn-stalks and grass stems with the utmost ease. The animal's tail is a great help to its owner when climbing, as this sensitive organ is prehensile, and can be wound about a corn-stalk to afford the harvest mouse extra support. No other British animal has such a prehensile tail.

It takes four harvest mice to turn the scales at one ounce, and of the many specimens which I have been privileged to handle an average of nine out of ten have been females. Many naturalist friends of mine tell me that their experiences have been similar, and only from one or two observers have reports come to the effect that, in their districts, the sexes seem to be equally numerous.

Unfortunately, the harvest mouse is of local

distribution only, and is entirely absent from certain districts of England. At the present time it is found chiefly in the south-eastern counties. It does not occur at all in Ireland, and in Scotland and the northern counties it is indeed rare. I am not aware of any authentic records of its appearing in Wales.

On the other hand, harvest mice often exist in fair numbers in districts where they are least suspected of being present, the probable reason being that they are not easily encountered. Not that they are more shy than other members of the mouse fraternity, nor yet that they more cleverly conceal themselves; quite the contrary, for the harvest mouse loves to be aloft, and is never happy for any length of time on the ground. Among growing corn is its favourite haunt, and to watch one of these dainty little creatures skilfully and quickly run up a corn stalk—its prehensile tail wrapped round the slender stalk, where it acts both as a safe anchorage and a balancer—is to witness one of Nature's acrobats at work. I have often seen these mice hang head downwards with the hind feet, or suspend themselves in that position by their tail. What is, perhaps, more amazing is the fact that the animal is able to twist itself back to the corn-stalk again with ease, and to continue its upward or downward run.

The greatest drawback to the would-be observer

of the harvest mouse is the often inaccessible territory which the animal favours. It is seldom possible for an observer to be allowed to walk through crops of growing corn—the most likely place to find the animals; and it is not always convenient to keep observation on corn-stacks, where the mice often gather in the autumn. Frankly, I can see little advantage in attempting to observe harvest mice in the latter environment, as to do so is not to see them under what may quite well be termed " natural " conditions. The home of the harvest mouse is the corn-field, and it is here that those who wish to see the animal at its best, and in the full glory of its acrobatic feats, must come.

A fact in favour of all observers is that the harvest mouse is more diurnal than nocturnal, and most of its activities are carried out by day. More than any other mouse it loves the sunshine, and I have often found four or five of them basking (and sometimes dozing) in the sun, usually huddled together on a stalk of corn, about two or three feet above ground. So light are they in weight that the corn stem does not even bend beneath its burden, and the tiny sleepers will sit there for hours if no one disturbs them.

If birds of prey had to depend on their catches of harvest mice for their livelihood they would soon know the pangs of hunger. Amid the corn these dainty little mice are singularly safe from the keen-eyed hunters of the air, which pounce with such certainty upon the other mice of the hedgerow, and the more clumsy voles, which so often wander from cover and protection. Of course, harvest mice are not exempt from enemies, for they have that sleek bandit, the weasel, to contend with, and also that bloodthirsty murderer, the stoat. Many must be the tragedies which these two animals exact among the harvest mice population—tragedies, which, because of the tall, waving corn amid which they are perpetrated, are unseen by human eye. Cats take toll of a few harvest mice, but not a great number, although I now recall that the last harvest mouse I saw was a dead specimen in the claws of a feline poacher.

Normally, harvest mice are gregarious and sociable, but occasions occur when, for some reason or other, certain individuals disagree, and from my observation it would appear that with this species old wounds never heal. A friend of mine who kept eight harvest mice in captivity for many months, found them most charming pets, and sociable with each other. They would crowd into a small dormitory at night, and after a chatter of little squeals—so peculiar to harvest mice— they would settle down in comfort for the night. My friend writes: " But one day a quarrel took place—the cause no one ever knew, but it was quite obvious which of the flock was the culprit; it was plainly seven against one, the latter being driven into a corner of the cage, while the others discussed matters. On the termination of this " Harvest Mice Court of Justice ", the culprit was killed and eaten.

The staple food of harvest mice is grain, but in common with most rodents they often eat insects, while berries and seeds are occasionally resorted to.

It has been stated by some naturalists that harvest mice hibernate, but my own observations do not corroborate this theory. It is true that they build winter nests in which, no doubt, they spend a great part of their lives asleep, but it is not the sleep of hibernation.

There is a tendency among harvest mice to lay up stores of food for winter shortage—another fact which tends to disprove the hibernation theory, and it would seem that this instinct is more pronounced in those mice that winter in the fields than with their brethren which select a corn-stack for their winter residence. This is not, perhaps, to be wondered at, for in a corn-stack it is more easy to find food than in the countryside.

The winter nests of harvest mice, to which I have already referred, are not easy to locate. Those which I have found (no more than half a dozen) have been either on the ground, carefully concealed in undergrowth, or below ground-level, and equally well concealed. The nests consist of leaves and blades of grass, shredded into strips and rolled together. There is no evidence of a systematic interweaving, and it is quite probable that the little animal constructs its winter nest in the same way as it does its breeding nest; that is, by pushing its way into the accumulation of grasses and leaves, and then, by turning round and round, forms the chamber which is to be its resting place, and, as regards its breeding nest, the nursery for the little ones, for it is in a nest such as this that harvest mice are born. The only difference is that the breeding nests of harvest mice are seldom, if ever, placed lower than two feet above the ground. Spherical in shape and about the size of a cricket-ball, these nests consist mainly of the leaves of the corn among which they are built, with the stalks as a scaffolding; the leaves used for these breeding nests are, as in the case of the animals' winter nests, shredded except for three or four whole leaves, which form the foundation of the fragile home. There is no recognized or observable entrance to the nest, but, owing to the elasticity of the materials used, the inhabitants are able to enter or leave their home by merely pushing their way through the structure, the aperture thus made immediately closing behind them.

The harvest mouse turns its attention to

41

domestic affairs in May or June, but the young are seldom born until the latter month, and, not infrequently, until later. July and August may well be regarded as the peak of the breeding period, although litters in September are not unusual. In spite of the short breeding season, however, the little animals manage to bring forth three or four litters with from five to eight (sometimes nine) young to each litter.

At birth the young are naked and blind, and incredibly tiny creatures; yet, in spite of their helplessness at birth, they develop so quickly that in about three weeks they are taking their first excursions up and down the corn-stalks.

Harvest mice make ideal pets if fed on a diet of oats and wheat, with canary seed, hemp, millet, rape and linseed added. They drink a great deal, and should never be without water. They soon become accustomed to dwelling in captivity, but anyone who has watched them displaying their gymnastic feats in the fields of waving corn cannot but feel that their heritage is freedom and not confinement.

HARVEST MOUSE

THE SHORT-TAILED FIELD VOLE

ALTHOUGH voles are rodents and often mistaken for rats and mice, there need be no confusion as to the identity of these two groups. It is only those folk not sufficiently interested to do more than just casually notice wild life that are unable to distinguish voles from rats and mice.

Voles are the more heavily and clumsily built of the two groups, with blunt muzzles, short ears which are almost hidden in fur; and, in the case of the vole concerned in this chapter, the short, stumpy tail is another clue to the identity of this animal. There are also differences in the habits of these two groups of rodents, for voles are less active than rats and mice, their legs are shorter, and they lack the ability to climb, so pronounced in their more agile relatives. Voles are less nocturnal than rats and mice, a fact which is evidenced by their smaller eyes, and are almost entirely vegetarian in their menu as compared with the omnivorous diet of the other groups of rodents.

The bank vole and the water vole also occur in this country, but they are less abundant than the

short-tailed field vole, and because of their haunts
—the former spending practically the whole of its
existence in moss or ivy-covered hedgerows and
banks, and the latter, being a creature of the
waterside—they do not come within the scope of
this present book.

The short-tailed field vole, however, loves the
open fields and pastures, where it often becomes
an easy prey for the kestrel or sparrow-hawk.
This vole has many alternative names, such as
common vole, grass vole, and meadow vole, while
to many it is known as the short-tailed field mouse.
In length the animal is little more than five inches,
of which about one inch is accounted for by the tail.

Field voles are gregarious by nature, and when
present in great numbers constitute a grave
danger to agriculture. Vole plagues have occurred
in the British Isles on several occasions, one of
the most serious on record having been in 1891–3,
when tremendous damage was done to crops,
pasture lands, and young trees. Lesser outbreaks
of vole plagues have occurred several times
since, and I remember seeing, some years ago,
a meadow which had been eaten bare by these
rodents; there was no grass at all left, and even
the hedgerows had been robbed of their herbage
as far up as the little rodents could reach. The
bark of trees had also been gnawed, and the
entire meadow had a most frightening appearance

44

of desolation. Voles appeared and disappeared on all sides with little concern for onlookers. It was a happy hunting-ground for stoats and weasels, and no doubt the kestrels had discovered this land of plenty. Few indeed are the opportunities for tasty meals which these hunters of the sky miss. Their keen eyes sight the slightest movement on the ground below, and before the vole, shrew or mouse realizes it has been seen, it is pounced upon, and once in the grip of the bird's talons the little victim's life swiftly comes to an end.

Vole plagues also occur in certain parts of the Continent, where thousands of acres are sometimes affected. These plagues have appeared from very ancient times, and it has been said that wet autumns and mild winters are conducive to the multiplication of voles.

No doubt a great amount of the mischief is due to the thoughtless and ruthless persecution of stoats, weasels, and birds of prey, all of which are the natural enemies of voles, and whose mission is to keep their numbers in check. It is a great pity that farmers and gamekeepers cannot be more discreet in their destruction of wild life; too often weasels and stoats are shot at sight, although, instead of being the farmer's enemies they are his allies. These two little bandits are no desirable guests in a game covert, but keepers often act equally unwisely in destroying certain species of owls, as well as the innocent hedgehog, which do more good than harm. This, however, does not satisfactorily explain vole plagues, nor why plagues should occur in some years and not in others. As a matter of fact, vole plagues often occur in the very districts where the vole's natural enemies are abundant, and it would seem that the most reasonable explanation of such plague outbreaks lies in some factor, or probably series of factors, that favour an enormous increase in the vole population.

Sheep and cattle often suffer seriously from insufficient pasture during vole plagues, and even when the plague has been abated the affected area is sometimes rendered unfit for cattle for months afterwards, owing to the terrible stench that arises from corpses which lie about in hundreds, especially if, as is sometimes the case, a disease breaks out among the vole population. Even apart from disease, stoats and weasels will kill for the sheer joy of killing, leaving hundreds of their victims to rot in the sun. In a vole-ridden area stoats and weasels do immense good in their wholesale slaughter of these little rodents.

In writing so fully concerning vole plagues, I have tried to stress the fact that it is not always the larger animals of our countryside which do the most damage, but the smaller, diminutive

46

creatures such as the voles and rabbits, which, although inoffensive and unostentatious, are capable of causing far more destruction and damage than foxes or badgers could ever do.

The short-tailed field vole is a timid, shy little creature, and seldom leaves cover if it can avoid doing so. It frequents open fields more than do its brethren, and constructs long runs in the grass. These runs are usually on and not below the surface, and are completely roofed over by the growing grass or herbage among which they are made, thereby completely hiding the animal from view. A run is not always easy to trace, but to open up one of these roadways is to be convinced of the active life lived by the voles. Except in the case of newly-made runs there is usually evidence of a well-worn track, suggesting long and frequent usage. The run itself is so completely roofed over by the lower portions of the grass stems which grow tightly together, that to disentangle them is often more than one's fingers can comfortably accomplish.

These vole " highways " are often a complicated network of tunnels, the shorter ones being used for frolic and games, and the longer ones—which often go for a considerable distance across the surface—are the voles' highways along which they travel to and from their feeding-grounds.

At one time and another I have examined many

of these runs. Very few are below ground-level, except in those cases where frequent use have worn them below surface. Croft land seems to suit voles best, for there the pasture is usually thick and close-growing, so that the little animals are able more easily to arch over their thoroughfares. These runs rather resemble those of the mole, in that there are many little culs-de-sac along the way, the purpose of which would seem to be to enable the travellers to move aside to allow another going in the opposite direction to proceed.

The best time to study the zigzag course of these runs is after the grass has been on fire—a not unusual occurrence in croft land—as the new grass is then sweeter and fresher. On recently burnt land it is easy to follow these vole highways and byways, and to learn more of their real nature and construction than at other times, although the fire makes them unusable for a long time, as a run without a roof is of little benefit to a vole. In the majority of cases, however, these runs are again tenanted and utilized when fresh pastures cover the once parched ground.

The short-tailed field vole lives underground, where it burrows holes in which to reside. More often than not these burrows are under cover or have some sort of protection from the weather. The roots of a tree or bush are often taken advantage of, and not infrequently the animal burrows its way beneath fallen trees, cattle troughs, stones, logs, or even chicken coops. I once found a vole residence beneath an old bucket that, after its mission as a scarecrow had been completed, was thrown into a hedgerow.

The animals are gregarious, several of them living peacefully together in the same burrow, but being shy and wary creatures, the short-tailed field voles are difficult to observe in their natural haunts. Their concealed runs lead right up to within a few inches of their burrow, so that the only chance one gets of studying them is the momentary pause they invariably make upon the threshold to their home or before entering their run. This pause is made to listen for danger, and, occasionally, to perform a hurried toilet.

They sometimes sit in the sun, but are always on the alert and are never more than a few inches from either their runs or their homes. The snapping of a twig, the rustle of a leaf, the startled call of a bird, and they disappear as if by magic. I have often been uncertain as to whether a frightened vole had taken to its run or to its burrow, so suddenly and rapidly has it vanished.

The field voles which I have been able to study in confinement and the few which I have been fortunate enough to observe in open pastures, have led me to form the conclusion that they never jump or leap. They are able to run quickly over a smooth surface, but are greatly handicapped on rough land, such as ground that has been recently ploughed. They are active both day and night, but indulge in frequent sleeps. In captivity they soon become reconciled and friendly; cases have been recorded of their rearing young in confinement, yet I think a vole is never really happy when imprisoned. Much of its docility is more the result of fear than affection, and although in many ways they are attractive, I really cannot understand anyone keeping them apart from the purpose of studying their behaviour and habits.

They do not hibernate, although in severe weather they seldom leave their burrows, where a wise instinct has prompted them to lay up stores of food against the winter shortage. Nothing in the way of hibernation is indulged in, and the reason why they come abroad less in winter is because they dislike wet or cold weather.

The young are usually born in the residential burrows of their parents, the female giving birth to from four to eight young in a litter. A nursery of grass awaits the young, and occasionally this may be found on the surface instead of underground. Breeding commences in April and continues until September or October, during which period many litters are produced, and it is highly probable that the earlier born young themselves breed before the year is done.

50

THE MYSTERIOUS CUCKOO

OF all our summer bird visitors the cuckoo is the most eagerly awaited. Old and young alike are always glad to hear the familiar " cuckoo, cuckoo " call-notes of this bird, for we know then that spring has really come.

Down through all the ages the cuckoo has been a bird of mystery, and in spite of the work of painstaking bird-lovers and naturalists, much of the bird's habits and life-history is still the subject of argument. I doubt if there is any other one bird about which such divergence of opinion exists. Nature photographers have, perhaps, done more than anyone else to record with indisputable proof some of the cuckoo's ways and habits, but even the camera cannot decide if all cuckoos act and live in the same way. The saying that " old notions die hard " is particularly true in relation to the cuckoo, and those folk who say that the cuckoo lays her egg on the ground and then carries it in her beak to her selected nest, argue that the fact that cameras have photographed cuckoos actually laying their eggs direct into the selected nest, does not necessarily prove that the old theory is wrong, for individual cuckoos may have different methods. So far as I am aware, however, no one has ever photographed a cuckoo in the act of carrying her own egg in her beak, but before discussing the nesting habits of this notable feathered visitor, perhaps it would be best to consider her arrival in Great Britain from Africa, where the winter is spent.

April brings the cuckoo to this country, the males usually arriving a few days ahead of the females. On their arrival, and for a few weeks afterwards, my observations tend to prove that the sexes do not associate. The male birds confine their movements to certain districts, while the females take up residence in other localities. They are shy, secretive birds, and but for their distinctive call-notes would probably be with us weeks before we are aware of their presence. Whilst writing of the cuckoo's call-notes I am reminded, upon reference to my field notes, that for the last five years I have first heard the cuckoo for each of those five years between the hours of eight and nine in the morning. I attach no importance to that fact, and merely quote it as being a singular coincidence.

Once having reached these shores, the birds may be heard from early morning until dusk. An old rhyme says that in May

He sings night and day,

52

and it is quite true that in that month the bird may be heard at a rather late hour. Whilst the " cuckoo, cuckoo " calls of these birds are familiar to all country dwellers, not everybody is so familiar with the " bubbling " calls which the female birds utter, yet these calls are just as frequently voiced as the more popular calls, especially during the mating season.

Like all migratory birds, the female cuckoos are in this country some weeks before laying. Their first duties, once they have turned their attention to domestic matters, is to select nests in which to lay their eggs, for it is common knowledge, and the one fact about cuckoos that is not disputed, that they build no nests of their own.

During the last six or seven years I have given special attention and devoted many hours of patient observation to this slate-grey visitor of spring which, when in flight, so closely resembles a kestrel that smaller birds tremble at its approach.

That the cuckoos' eggs are hatched out and the young reared by other birds is agreed by all, but the method by which the female cuckoos get their eggs into those nests is a question about which, as I have already mentioned, much divergence of opinion exists.

There are at least three different theories: the first and oldest being that the bird lays her egg on the ground and then carries it in her beak to the selected nest; the second theory—and the most widely accepted at the moment—is that the cuckoo lays her egg direct into the nest in the same way as any other bird would do; whilst the third theory, denying neither of the two already mentioned, suggests that both those methods are adopted according to individual choice.

Of the first method, although it is the oldest theory, we have little or no proof, but of the fact that the cuckoo lays her egg direct into the selected nest we have ample evidence by way of photographs and cinematograph films. The third theory, that the cuckoo sometimes adopts one method and sometimes another is, of course, within the bounds of possibility, but without any foundation in fact.

Of the many instances which have come under my personal observation, I have never once seen a cuckoo lay her egg anywhere except direct into the chosen nest. But I have seen many a cuckoo carrying an egg in her beak—but not her own egg, it being her practice to steal an egg from the rightful owners of the nest which she victimizes before laying her own.

Probably it is those stolen eggs which those observers who cling to the ancient belief have seen cuckoos carrying, thus giving rise to the old theory.

YOUNG CUCKOO IN WILLOW WREN'S NEST

My observations of the cuckoo brands the bird as a thief, for whilst she lays only on alternate days, I have seen her steal eggs from the same nest each day in succession until there was only one egg left—and that the cuckoo's own. The victimized bird was an innocent hedge accentor (commonly, though wrongly, called hedge " sparrow "), yet she incubated the cuckoo's egg without demur and later attended to the needs of the offspring as if it were her own. Long before this young pirate left the nest it was much bigger than its foster-parents.

For a number of years I have kept observation on a meadow which cuckoos frequent annually. Early in April I erect a small " hide ", consisting of gorse and herbage, from which to keep watch. Searching the hedges to locate the nests of birds which are likely to be victimized I await the movements of the cuckoo.

By the middle of April several cuckoos have visited the meadow, carefully searching the hedges for nests in which to lay their eggs when the time arrives. Among the usual nests in the meadow were hedge accentors, pied wagtails, and meadow pipits, all of which are frequently utilized by cuckoos.

Having selected her nest, the cuckoo visits it frequently until she is ready to lay her egg. If the selected nest is only in course of construction, she seems to take more interest than usual in it. Four or five visits a day are often made, to the annoyance of the busy builders.

It is not unusual for a cuckoo to choose a nest in course of construction, but I have never known her to lay her egg before there is at least one of the rightful owner's laid. Neither have I known a cuckoo lay an egg in a nest where the eggs already laid were being incubated. This credits the bird with remarkable forethought, for were she to lay her egg under such circumstances the other eggs would hatch first, and the young fledglings probably be too large to be brutally treated in the way young cuckoos treat their nest-fellows.

My observations show that before actually laying her egg the cuckoo enjoys a period of rest —a period which varies from half an hour to three, or even four hours. There is nothing unusual about this, as it is a characteristic of all birds, the only difference being that the cuckoo rests on some convenient perch, while other birds sit in their nests before laying.

When the cuckoo is ready to lay she flies to the selected nest and cautiously forces her way through gorse or bracken in order first to reach one of the eggs of the rightful owners. This egg the cuckoo holds in her beak until she has laid her own egg direct into the nest. The actual laying takes only about a minute, after which she glides back to a perch (usually the one she recently left) and eats the stolen egg.

During the many years which I have devoted to the study of wild birds I have been privileged to observe some twenty odd instances of female cuckoos laying their eggs, and in each case the method adopted has been precisely the same. The species of birds victimized have differed, and wagtails, yellow buntings, meadow pipits, tree pipits and reed warblers have been among the birds chosen for foster parents.

Cuckoos lay on alternate days and their eggs vary in appearance; the most usual description being brownish-red spots on a grey surface. The eggs are distinctly out of place among the bright, greenish-blue eggs of the hedge accentor, yet this little bird is frequently victimized by the cuckoo, and the strangest thing about it is that the hedge accentor does not object to the strange-looking egg, although its presence among her own must be noticed. The eggs are more in harmony with the appearance of the pied wagtail's than those of any other bird whose nest the cuckoo utilizes, which is, perhaps, why the wagtails are so often entrusted with the arduous and unpleasant task of rearing young cuckoos.

After the laying of her eggs the cuckoo continues to visit the different nests in which they are laid to see that all goes well with them. The number of eggs which each female cuckoo lays in a season is difficult to ascertain, but the probability is that if any of her eggs are stolen or come to grief she goes on laying until a full complement is being safely incubated.

The period of incubation is about thirteen days, and when the young cuckoo hatches a life-story is enacted which is without equal among all the feathered fraternity, and one of the most interesting ever recorded in the annals of natural history.

At birth the impudent youngster is naked and blind. For the first day all goes well, and the baby cuckoo peacefully nestles among its nest-fellows, but on the second or third day the young feathered pirate becomes restless and remarkably strong. It refuses to tolerate the presence of the other fledglings and, disregardful of their legitimate right to the nursery, proceeds to eject them.

Working its way to the bottom of the nest, the young cuckoo shuffles and twists until it succeeds in getting on to its back one of the other fledglings. Then gradually rising on its legs the cuckoo raises its burden until it is level with the top of the nest, when a slight effort is all that is needed in order to send the innocent infant to its doom. All the cuckoo's nest-fellows

YOUNG CUCKOO

are treated similarly, as also are any unhatched eggs, and after making quite sure that it is the sole occupant of the nursery the young tyrant settles down.

Strangely enough—and to my mind it is one of the strangest facts of bird-life—the foster parents on their return to the nest take no notice whatever of the tragedy that has befallen their family, and devote the whole of their attention to the young cuckoo as if it had been their own offspring. I remember once watching a pair of wagtails return to their nest to find that, during their absence, a young cuckoo had ejected their two chicks, both of which lay wriggling on the ground beneath, yet the wagtails — normally among the most devoted of bird parents—took not the slightest notice and quite callously allowed the young chicks to die.

The task of the fosterers, however, in undertaking the rearing of the young cuckoo, is heavy, for it is a gluttonous baby, ever clamouring for food, and unless it is regularly fed becomes very disagreeable. Its food consists chiefly of insects and grubs, and even after it has flown the devoted fosterers continue to follow and feed it. The small foster parents are kept continuously at work in order to find sufficient food for their big baby, and it is quite certain that if the young cuckoo did not eject its nest-fellows the parents

59

would never have been able to rear them all; moreover, the nest could not accommodate them, for long before the cuckoo leaves its nursery it has to sit *on*, rather than *in*, it.

Somehow or other the fledgling cuckoo seems to be a favourite among the feathered population, and I have often seen other birds, while on their way to feed their own young, stop to give a tit-bit to a young cuckoo. I have seen whitethroats and buntings feed a young cuckoo that was reared in a meadow pipit's nest.

Adult cuckoos do not pair as most other birds do; they are, by nature, polyandrous, and in July they leave these shores for warmer climes.

Young cuckoos, however, sojourn here for some weeks after the adults have gone, which goes to prove that they need no pilots to guide them, young though they be, on their long flight southward.

THE PARTRIDGES

THE common partridge is essentially a bird of the fields, and in every sense of the word it is a true Englishman. For many, many years it has been associated with the English countryside, where it is well known to farmers, sportsmen, gamekeepers, naturalists, and even to the occasional country rambler.

It is a gregarious bird and moves about in companies, or to use the proper term, " coveys ". It has remarkable protective coloration, and by remaining motionless in its natural environment, it is usually passed by unnoticed.

I have often watched a covey of partridges settle, and yet be unable to locate one of them a moment after. Knowing that the birds must be in a certain field, it is very interesting to walk over the land endeavouring to locate them. The chances are, however, that you will fail until the covey suddenly rises on noisy wings a few inches in front of your very feet.

Partridges were amongst the birds to which I first devoted my study and observation. On the farm where I spent my boyhood the land suited them well, and many broods were raised in our fields year after year. They are not difficult to study once their nest is found, and the hen, being such a close sitter, will allow one's near approach to her nest before leaving it. One instance which stands out in my memory clearly is that of a sitting partridge which nested amid the growing hay and refused to leave her nest when the hay was being cut. No one knew of the sitting bird until the knives of the mower had mutilated her body and she lay between the ranks of the new-mown hay, a mass of blood and bedraggled feathers. Her ten eggs lay in the nest undamaged—undisturbed, it seemed, and when discovered were still warm from the heat of the bird's body.

At home I had a broody bantam to whose care I carefully removed the eggs. She brooded them as if they had been her very own, and eventually hatching day arrived and every one of the eggs gave birth to a chick—lovely and attractive little creatures, warmly clothed in a coat of brownish down streaked with black and darker brown.

Then came the problem of feeding them, for in a wild state young partridges are fed largely on insects. In about an hour after birth they were quite active, and it was thought best to remove them with their foster-mother, to a field where they might be able to find some insect fare for themselves. A coop was made and the proud mother and her family transferred to the hayfield in which the mother partridge had so tragically met her fate; but before evening of that day every chick had gone. Rats, stoats, weasels, birds of prey, all became " suspects " until, some evenings later, the ten youngsters were seen with their father, feeding in the hedgerow. Later on, some people who were camping in an adjoining field told us how they watched the old partridge fearlessly approach the coop and encourage the chicks one by one away from their foster-mother to follow him and live a normal partridge's life.

I have known partridges reared under domestic conditions, but they seldom make the happy, shrewd and cautious partridges of the fields. To study wild partridges is to marvel at their amazing instinct and cunning (to which I shall refer in more detail later on in this chapter), but partridges reared in farmyards seem to lack much of the attractiveness and, shall I call it " field-craft ", of wild birds. Instead of doing their best to avoid detection and cautiously taking cover when observed, as do the partridges of the fields, these semi-domesticated birds walk boldly and stupidly about the orchard or garden—whichever happens to be their private domain—quite unconcerned for their own safety.

I think the explanation is that birds reared under domestic conditions naturally receive no training from their foster-mother, and that their natural instincts are not encouraged to develop. It is far different with those chicks whose good fortune it is to have the wise counsel, guidance and instruction of a mother partridge. No bird is more devoted to her family than the partridge, and her husband, too, is equally attentive to his progeny. In common with all ground and game birds, partridges have many natural enemies, and young partridges are singularly fortunate in having wise parents to instil into their young minds how best to escape the many perils which are their common lot as birds of our fields.

In spite of their many natural enemies, however, mankind takes toll of more partridges than do all the predatory creatures of the countryside put together.

As a table bird the partridge is regarded a luxury. In September partridge shooting begins, and then many and frequent are the tragedies of the partridge coveys. The birds' only safety lies in taking cover, and if fields of standing corn are available, they prove the partridges' salvation. Shooting, however, seldom begins in real earnest until corn has been cut, when the partridges' chief security is in fields of roots. Dogs and beaters are employed to disturb the birds from their hiding-places whilst the " guns " await the rising of the birds. By the autumn large coveys of partridges are usual, and it is surprising out of the large flock which face the guns how many survive. Unfortunately, however, the survivors are followed to their resting-places and again disturbed so that by the end of a day's shoot, sunset sees but a remnant of the covey that welcomed the sunrise.

When disturbed, partridges rise noisily on quivering wings and then glide on motionless wings, slightly curved downward, to their next resting-place. Their call-notes are difficult to describe, being coarse, scratchy, creaking sounds usually heard most frequently in the evenings from May onwards.

The partridge is, in shape, very rotund, short-tailed and brownish above with a greyish-coloured breast, on which is a dark horse-shoe shaped mark; the throat and chest are reddish-brown with a tendency for the males to have a brighter appearance than females. Sexing, however, is difficult unless one is able to handle the birds. Some writers say that the male birds have a more erect carriage when walking than females, but whilst this has appeared to be true in some instances, I do not think it a reliable method of sexing.

Partridges walk quickly, and are able to run

at a great speed. Through fields of growing corn or hay they have their recognized routes, and if a partridge can run to safety it much prefers doing so to taking flight.

In February much activity begins among partridges, as the return of spring days directs their thoughts to domestic affairs and the males begin seeking partners. As is often the case, two males frequently pay their attentions to the same fair lady, with the result that much quarrelling takes place. The two rivals chase each other round and round and round until the weaker of the two gets too tired to continue. Sometimes a fight follows, in which the weaker bird becomes badly plucked and beaten. I have never known these fights end fatally, but I have known instances in which one determined male has so relentlessly persecuted and pursued another, that the latter has taken shelter in chickens' coops, farm outbuildings, and, on one occasion, in a garden greenhouse. The victor, of course, wins the fair lady, and the vanquished, later on, finds an equally good partner, and by April nearly all partridges are in pairs.

It is some weeks, however, before eggs are laid, and I seldom discover any until the first week in May. Occasionally eggs are found in April, but I would prefer to put early in May as the most general time of laying.

ENGLISH PARTRIDGES (COCK AND HEN)

NEST OF RED-LEGGED PARTRIDGE

The hen bird selects a hollow or depression in which to lay her eggs; sometimes in a well-concealed position in a hedgerow, and at other times in growing corn or hay. Instances have been recorded of the birds coming to nest in gardens and orchards, but such instances are the exception rather than the rule.

No nest is made for the reception of the eggs, but it would seem as if some kind of lining is added after the hen has commenced laying. I have often seen the two birds bringing grass stems to their nest when eggs are already in it. When the young leave the nursery there is a definite lining of grasses and leaves in the hollow.

The number of eggs a partridge lays to a clutch varies; ten is usual, but thirteen and fourteen are not infrequent, and cases of twenty have been reported, although these were probably the result of two hens laying in one nest. The eggs are carefully covered after laying until the hen sits. In colour the eggs are pale olive-green, and closely match their surroundings. The sitting partridge, herself, however, is a far better example of protective coloration, her beautifully pencilled brown plumage harmonizing so perfectly with her surroundings that she is difficult to detect.

Once she has commenced incubation she becomes very bold, and will even allow herbage to be parted in order to photograph her, and many instances have been recorded of people stroking sitting partridges without the birds leaving their eggs.

Unlike the male pheasant, which is a worthless husband, the male partridge is an ideal mate, devoted in the extreme to his wife and constantly taking her tit-bits of food during the incubation period. He is never far away when the eggs are hatching, and as soon as the young have been born and are dry he and his wife lead them out into the fields.

Partridges often employ all sorts of tactics in order to divert one's attention from their nest or little ones. I was recently walking through a meadow when a partridge emerged from the hedgerow, ran a few yards ahead, and then dropped over on its side. It gave me the impression of a broken wing or injured leg and I went speedily to where the bird lay to take it up. When about a foot from the spot, the partridge moved on again in the same limping way. I followed, and this stratagem was repeated until the far end of the meadow had been reached, when away flew the partridge satisfied that its work had been well done. I later discovered that well hidden in the hedgerow, close to the place from where the bird had emerged, was his partner incubating a dozen eggs.

68

Similar tactics are used to divert an outsider's attention from the brood, the parents remaining close to the trespasser and doing all sorts of things to draw his attention. Meanwhile the chicks are conscious of the presence of danger and lie motionless on the ground, where their protectively-coloured fluffy brown plumage serves them in good stead.

There is another partridge now fairly common in certain parts (more particularly in the southern districts) of England. It is the French, or red-legged partridge, a bird which was introduced into this country rather more than a hundred years ago. It is more brightly coloured than our common partridge, having bright red beak and legs; its black eye-stripes form a necklace over a white throat, its blue-grey sides being prominently barred with black and brownish-red.

Nesting habits are similar; but I have never found the eggs of the red-legged partridge covered prior to incubation as is the case with our common partridge.

O F our two British larks—the skylark and the woodlark—the former is the more widely distributed, occurring throughout the British Isles, where it is everywhere loved for its beautiful and melodious song.

Although dressed in a sombre plumage of browns and greys, the skylark has, down through the ages, been the inspiration of many fine poems. It is well termed

" the bird that soars on highest wing ",

for to every countryside dweller the silver-toned song of this bird—uttered at such a height from the ground that the songster is often invisible—is as familiar as the sunrise. Indeed, I rather think that it is in early morning when the golden rays of the rising sun creep into the eastern sky, that the skylark sings at its very best and sweetest.

Its glorious song, however, although most frequently uttered on the wing, is occasionally poured forth whilst the bird is on the ground, and sometimes whilst perching on some low hedge or post. The skylark sings throughout the year, except in August, but spring and summer are the most favoured months for song. Weather does not affect the feathered songster, and I have often heard the bird's clear, sweet notes during a thunder-storm, when the minstrel itself could not be seen against the darkened sky. Nightingales also often sing well during thunder-storms, but I have noticed that the majority of bird songsters are silent on such occasions.

The skylark is a lover of the open fields and meadows, and is able to run over its grassy play-ground very quickly. It possesses, in common with the partridge, the power and instinct to conceal itself, and a skylark is just as difficult as a partridge to see against a grassy background. I have often watched a skylark drop through the air like a stone, breaking its descent when only a few feet from the ground, then to glide on to the pastures. Keeping my eye—or aided by field-glasses—focused on the spot where the bird alighted, I have made my way direct to the place to find no trace of the skylark. The bird may, of course, be squatting within arm's reach, or it may have dodged its way through the grass to some distant point from which, in a few minutes, it will rise again into the air. The bird sings as it rises and I have timed a skylark singing without a break for twenty-eight minutes, during which time the songster kept aloft on quivering wings.

Because of its vocal ability the skylark was at one time in great demand by bird catchers, who caught the birds and sold them. Many a genuine bird-lover's heart has bled to see these champion songsters in small wicker cages in London bird shops selling at half-a-crown each. Of recent years, however, the Wild Birds Protection Acts have done much to give the skylark more freedom from such practices. I am quite aware that many a caged skylark sings as well as its wild brethren, but the skylark is, I think, more so perhaps than any other bird, a bird of the open sky.

In early spring, when the pairing season approaches, the male birds quarrel frequently among themselves and fight many a battle. After sighting each other the two combatants usually rise into the air simultaneously, meet and drop to the ground in each other's grip. No real harm comes of these squabbles, and by March the troubles are usually over.

The nest, composed of grass and roots, is placed on the ground, the bird selecting a slight depression, usually well hidden by long grass or herbage. It is an open, cup-shaped nest in which from three to five eggs are laid. The nest, because of the materials which compose it, is difficult to detect, and the greyish-brown mottled eggs do not assist the seeker.

The skylark seldom drops direct to its nest,

preferring to alight some distance away and then stealthily to approach its home by some concealed and well-recognized route. Should someone be watching, the skylark is most careful not to betray the whereabouts of its nest, and will thread its way through the grass for some distance rather than alight near the site. Similarly, when leaving home, the bird often runs a few yards before going aloft.

At birth the young are covered with a hairy down and are rather queer-looking babies. They, too, when lying huddled together in their nursery, enjoy protective coloration, and are usually silent except when they welcome with shrill squeals the approach of their mother or father with food. The young leave the nest before they are able to fly, and are adept at taking cover when alarmed or in danger.

Both the skylark and the woodlark possess head-crests which they are able to erect or lower at will. These crests are usually prominent when the birds are running over the ground or when engaged in squabbles with each other.

The wood lark is a small edition of the skylark, although it possesses a longer and more prominent crest. In spite of its name it is not a bird of the woods, preferring the fields, heathlands and commons. It closely resembles the tree pipits, but its crest and shorter tail help to identify the bird.

The nest is built on the ground in similar situations to those used by skylarks, but it is a more compact and neater structure than that of its relative. The four or five eggs are rather like those of the skylark, but are more reddish in colour and are usually found earlier in the year.

The woodlark is quite a good songster, but its notes are not so varied or so sweet as the skylark's.

I do not know who first called the meadow pipit the " titlark ", but such is the name by which the demure little bird is locally known. It is rather interesting to learn these local names of birds, for many of them are very aptly appropriated, such as for instance, the green woodpecker being called the " Yaffle ", because of its singing laugh-like call, and the pipistrelle bat being known as the " Flittermouse ".

The meadow pipit is widely distributed throughout the British Isles, and wherever there are fields and meadows there you will find this sombrely clad little bird.

The nest is made on the ground under shelter of herbage or in a depression under a stone, and is composed of grasses with a lining of softer materials. Four or five eggs are laid, not unlike those of the skylark, being of a mottled greenish-brown appearance but smaller than the skylark's eggs and also smaller than those of the tree pipit, which they also resemble.

SKYLARK: REMOVING EXCREMENT

WOOD LARK AND YOUNG

The meadow pipit's eggs may be looked for in April, and the bird is frequently victimized by the cuckoo. Although the nest is well hidden, the meadow pipit often betray the secret of its whereabouts by their excited behaviour whenever one comes close to the site. The bird flits up and down around the intruder in great agitation, uttering its piping call-notes and plainly saying that no one has any right to trespass within such close range of its nest. On such occasions one is advised to tread very carefully until a safe distance from the forbidden territory—a fact which is soon made evident by the birds' more restful behaviour.

Such ground-nesting birds suffer cruelly from the ravages of stoats, weasels, mice and voles, while the keen-eyed kestrel has wrecked many a meadow pipit's home.

The tree pipit is another member of the pipit family which also nests on the ground, but it frequents the open woodlands rather than the fields, and has been dealt with elsewhere.[1] Yet another member of this clan is the rock pipit, a bird of the sand-dunes and sea-shore.

[1] *At Home in the Woods.*

THE FINCHES

THE finches are a very attractive group of birds, comprising some of the most handsome and beautifully coloured of our feathered denizens. I do not think that anywhere in this land of ours can we find two more pretty birds than the goldfinch and the bullfinch.

The goldfinch, until wild bird legislation came to the rescue, was in grave danger of extinction, so greatly was it sought after by bird catchers. In addition to its lovely plumage of different shades of brown and grey, with rich yellow wing-bars and crimson head-patch, it is a first-rate songster, and has frequently bred in captivity. Of recent years, however, the goldfinch has become more abundant, with the result that it is fairly well established once again.

We cannot afford to lose this handsome bird from our fields, where to see a flock of them feeding from a thistle patch, every now and then taking a short flight from one thistle to another, or indulging in aerial display, their bright golden wing-bars glittering in the sunlight, is to witness

one of the loveliest sights which our fields have
to offer.

After many years of patient study and observation of British birds in various parts of our
beloved country, there is no bird which holds
such fascination for me as the goldfinch. Every
movement, every action of the goldfinch is graceful and no other bird seems to possess such happy
abandon coupled with a delicacy of movement.
Their glorious colours certainly add to their
charm, and I often wondered whether if goldfinches were drab little birds, they would still
hold the same fascination for me. No lover of
birds could help admiring the goldfinch's beauty
and gracefulness, but perhaps my great admiration
for them dates back to my boyhood days and
to the home of my youth, where goldfinches were
abundant. When I was about eight years old I
rescued a goldfinch from the claws of a cat, and
later found that she was the mother of four
fledglings almost ready to leave their mossy home
in a nearby elder tree. The unfortunate bird
sustained a broken wing, and it was most pathetic
to watch the devoted husband bring food to the
cage in which we placed her. Then we became
anxious for the welfare of the young, for they
were continually calling for food and, what was
still worse, their calls had attracted the attention
of the cat. It was evident that the father bird

was unable to cope with the needs of these four extra mouths in addition to attending to his sick wife, so we decided to remove the young into the cage with their mother, in the hope that from the food there provided she would be able to help out her husband. The moment we dropped the nest in the cage the four fledglings left it and flew madly about their prison in terrific excitement; a few chirps from their mother, however, soon reconciled them, and when father next visited the cage he had the whole family to greet him. The mother helped him, however, and ate freely from the groundsel and other natural food which we supplied until the young were safe to be liberated. It was amusing to watch these youngsters enjoying their newly-found wing-power, but in spite of having their freedom they frequently visited their mother in her cage in the lilac tree. Eventually, mother was also given her freedom, and although her wing was by no means as strong as formerly, she managed to keep out of harm's way.

Goldfinches are rather late breeders, seldom beginning to nest until May. Their cup-shaped nest is neatly made of moss and lichen, cosily lined with hair and feathers. The materials used for the walls of the nest are strongly interwoven, the builders taking great care to use moss and lichen which harmonize with their immediate

surroundings. No attempt is made to conceal
the nest, and the most exposed positions are often
utilized, yet so perfect is the natural camouflage
of the home that it is one of the most difficult
nests to discover. The chaffinch also practices
this natural camouflage, as we shall see later on
in this chapter.

The goldfinch nests in trees; it loves the
orchard for nesting purposes and apple trees are
great favourites, but elders, privet, firs and holly
are also used, and not infrequently gorse bushes
are the site chosen by these dainty birds.

Four to six eggs are laid, pale greenish-white
in ground colour, thinly spotted with reddish-
brown. In the early days of their life the young
are fed mainly on insects, the parents swallowing
the food themselves and then regurgitating it into
the mouths of the chicks. When old enough the
young are fed on seeds of wild plants—chickweed,
groundsel, thistle and so forth—and in this respect
goldfinches have an economic value to farmers and
gardeners. Two broods are reared in a year.

When the young leave the nest they are known
as " greypates " because of their slate-grey attire.
Adults and young flock together in late summer
and autumn, but often return to the same nesting
sites year after year.

Whilst the sexes of goldfinches, because of their
almost identical plumage, are most difficult to

determine, the bullfinches are quite the reverse. The male bullfinch, with his carmine breast and glossy black cap, is indeed a handsome and stately gentleman, but his wife lacks the crimson adornment of her husband and is a sombrely clad lady, but none the less a dutiful and devoted wife.

Unfortunately, the bullfinch is no friend or ally of the gardener. I wish I could plead in its favour, but there is nothing to commend its presence in gardens and orchards, except, of course, the beauty and the attractive ways of the bird. These points, however, no matter how commendable in themselves, would not compensate the gardener for the damage which the bullfinch does to fruit trees and bushes.

It is of a shy and retiring disposition, but because of its bright plumage the male bird is not easily overlooked. Then the plaintive piping call-notes of both sexes is a ready identification, and cannot be confused with the calls of any other British bird.

Few mated birds are more devoted to each other than bullfinches, and to watch a pair of these birds attending to their domestic duties, in spite of the fact that in cultivated areas they are destructive sinners, is to win one's love and admiration for them.

Some years ago I found a half-fledged nestling by the wayside, and although I closely scanned the surrounding trees and bushes no sign of the nest from which it had come could be seen. It was rather a mystery—a mystery that was never explained—why this youngster should be left neglected and alone in a country lane. The chances are that someone had taken the nest and its contents to hand-rear them, and that this one had escaped. However, it could not be left there to perish, and so I took it home. At this stage of its existence it looked nothing like a bullfinch, being dressed in a grey garb with very little of interest about it. But I recognized it to be a young "bully", and in spite of the many jeers that were thrown at me for trying to rear a "hedge-sparrow" or a "wagtail", I proceeded to feed this young waif. To hand-rear birds is not easy; they have to be fed properly, regularly and often. I do not recommend it to anyone except under special circumstances. However, this fledgling responded to my treatment and grew into a fine male bullfinch. Although it was given the freedom of the garden, the bird remained a lovable pet, and would come to my hand for food. But it had an untimely end; its dead body was found on the garden path with no sign of mutilation or injury, and an open verdict was recorded.

The nest of the bullfinch is a frail and loosely made structure of twigs and weed stalks lined with roots and hair. Its situation is usually a shady one in the centre of a thick bush or tree; blackthorn is a tree often used, but nests in firs are also common. In fact the dark recesses of any tree suit the bullfinch well and a height of from five to seven feet is the most usual position for a nest. The four to six greenish-blue eggs are spotted with black and brown and may be found in April.

Normally, a brooding hen bullfinch will sit closely until actually forced to leave her nest; she is an admirable subject for photography although, owing to the shady situations in which her nest is placed, the photographer still has the consequent drawbacks to contend with. Two broods are sometimes reared, though this is not an invariable characteristic of the bullfinch, but I believe the birds pair for life, the mated pairs often remaining together throughout the year, and although they are sociable birds, large flocks of bullfinches are unusual.

The greenfinch is another member of the finch clan, and a bird which, in spite of its dull olive-green plumage, has a beauty and a neatness all its own. It has no song to boast about, and although it may make an occasional theft from the garden it cannot be classed as a bad offender. Greenfinches sometimes favour fruit trees for nesting sites, but they haunt almost any type of

GOLDFINCH AT NEST

country, being just as much at home in the fields and commons as anywhere else.

It is one of the commonest of British birds, and in autumn and winter large flocks of them may be seen haunting fields and stack-yards. Chaffinches sometimes consort with them, and such assemblages not infrequently number hundreds of birds.

The greenfinch is a bird of stout build, and well able to hold its own in a fight even with some birds thrice its size. Anyone who possesses a feeding-table will have witnessed the pugnacious character of the bird and how easily it puts blackbirds and song thrushes to flight, not to mention the many scares it gives the tits and smaller birds.

Greenfinches subsist chiefly on seeds, and are particularly fond of berries. Autumn is their season of plenty, the hips of the wild roses and the berries of the elders claiming much of their attention. The young are fed by regurgitation, and when incubating the hen is also fed in this way by her partner.

Nesting commences early in the year and sometimes three broods are raised in a season. The nest consists of a platform of fine twigs cemented together with moss, on which the nest proper is built. Moss, lichen, wool and roots are used in its construction, with a lining of finer materials.

The finished structure looks loose and untidy, but it is deceiving in its appearance and actually is a strongly made piece of work. Evergreens are frequently used for nesting sites, but the bird has no distinct preference, and wherever a shady and well-concealed site is available there the greenfinch builds its home. I believe the hen bird does most of the building, her mate bringing her the materials.

From four to six eggs are laid, long in shape, greenish-white in colour, spotted and streaked at the larger end with purplish-brown. The eggs are inclined to vary in appearance, and have sometimes been confused with those of other finches. The young develop quickly and the majority of broods are on the wing within about a fortnight from hatching; their streaked plumage is well adapted for concealment.

Next in this group comes the chaffinch, a bird in which the sexes differ in appearance as greatly as do the bullfinches. The male chaffinch is a bold, smart-looking bird with pale chestnut breast, blue-grey head and white wing-bars, whilst the hen bird is dull greyish-green in colour and lacks entirely the brightly coloured breast of the male, although she has equally prominent white wing-bars.

The chaffinch is widely distributed throughout the British Isles, where its " pink, pink " call-notes are familiar to country and town dwellers alike. It frequents all kinds of country—fell, woods, commons, marshes, orchards, gardens—and is often seen in towns and thickly populated areas. It is a bird which shows remarkable boldness, especially in winter, when shortage of food drives it to our homesteads and gardens.

I know of no more grateful bird; every kindness is rewarded by a series of " pinks ", and the male bird possesses quite a cheery little song, which he proudly utters. The chaffinch is amongst the earliest of British birds to resume its song after the winter. The song thrush is probably the earliest of all to welcome with its melodious voice the longer days of February, but the male chaffinch in its more simple way is a close rival.

It is also one of the earliest of the finch family to nest, and February not infrequently sees the chaffinches choosing their partners. The marvellously constructed nest of this bird is considered by many naturalists and observers the finest example of British bird architecture. It certainly is a wonderful achievement, for which the hen bird merits the entire credit, but it is difficult to decide whether to give first place to the nest of the chaffinch or to that of the long-tailed tit. Both are wonderful examples of avian architecture, being strongly and neatly made of moss and lichen, closely interwoven and lavishly lined with hair and feathers. The exterior of the nest is often decorated with moss and lichen from the branch on which it is placed, thus making the natural camouflage perfect. So strongly is the nest made that it is difficult to pull it to pieces with one's fingers. When sitting in her nest the greenish back of the hen bird tones excellently well with her environment, and is no help whatever to locating her mossy home. She is a very close sitter, and does not leave her nest until one almost touches her. I have often touched the nest with my fingers before the hen moved off. When thus disturbed she and her husband become very agitated, flying about in great excitement and calling loudly until the danger has passed.

Four or five eggs are laid—occasionally six—these being greenish - grey in ground colour, blotched with reddish - brown, spotted with brownish-black. The markings vary greatly both in colour and position, but the eggs are usually so distinctive as to be easily recognizable.

When the young leave the nest they are almost exact replicas of their mother, and it is only after the first moult that the male birds assume their more gaudily coloured attire. Two broods are raised in a year, and the same nesting sites are often used in successive years.

The largest member of the finch family is the

hawfinch, a bird less numerous than the finches we have considered. Its distribution covers practically the whole of England and includes the southern part of Scotland and some parts of Wales. It is decidedly the most shy and retiring of the finch family—and probably the shyest of all our British birds. It frequents two types of country—the tall hedges of fields and the woods, but wherever its territory, it is a bird of the trees and is seldom seen. I regard it as a silent bird, and its stout build and strong, wedge-shaped beak give it a forbidding appearance. The bird is able to inflict a hard blow, as I once learned to my bitter experience, through carelessly handling a show specimen.

On the inside the hawfinch's large beak is furnished with hard knobs to enable its owner to crunch the stones of fruit—especially plum and cherry, so as to extract the kernels. In gardens and orchards the hawfinch is never tolerated, and one of the bird's weaknesses is pea-stealing. A whole crop of green peas is stolen in a few hours, the empty pods being left strewn about the ground as evidence of what once was.

The nest of the hawfinch is composed of small twigs and roots, lined with finer roots and hair, and is usually placed in a tree at a considerable height from the ground and well concealed. It is a flat, loosely-made structure, and when the five or six chicks are half-fledged it looks none too secure. However, I have never known one to come to grief, and the fact that many of them are in position the following spring, having withstood the winter's gales, proves that they are firmer and better made than they appear to be. The eggs are greenish-white in ground colour with reddish and purplish-brown markings and blotches.

Another attractive little bird of the fields and belonging to the finch family is the linnet. The hen bird is an ideal housekeeper, keeping the nest clean and tidy even when there are young to be fed, and although in her drab and streaked attire she is not so brightly coloured as her mate in his rosy-hued breast and cap, no bird is more devoted to the interests and welfare of her home and family.

In autumn and winter flocks of linnets haunt open fields, and although the bird is gregarious at this time of year it is none too sociable with its own clan during the breeding season. Sometimes, because of the availability of nesting sites three or four nests are found comparatively close together, but very little neighbourliness exists among the respective pairs, and each wedded couple keeps strictly to its own territory.

The linnet is a fairly early breeder, and by the middle of April nesting is in full swing.

Gorse bushes are greatly favoured as nesting sites, the birds making a neat nest of fine twigs, grass and wool, with a cosy lining of hair. As a rule the nest is well hidden and about five or six feet from the ground. The four or five pale greenish-white eggs are thinly spotted with reddish-brown, and are rather fragile looking. Two broods are raised in a season.

Belonging to the same genus are the mealy and the lesser redpolls. Taking the last first, the lesser redpoll somewhat resembles its close relative, the linnet, but may be distinguished by its brighter crimson crown and forehead and by a black throat patch. It frequents trees more than do linnets, and frequently nests at a greater height. The nest is neatly constructed of fine twigs and roots; in appearance it is similar to that of the linnet, but the redpoll prefers a lining of vegetable down to the hair lining of the linnet's nest. The eggs, four to six in number, closely resemble the linnets', but show more variation in ground colour, which may be of a pale blue, and sometimes the markings are more thickly distributed.

The mealy redpoll does not breed in this country, but visits us in the winter, when large flocks of them may be seen frequenting fields and commons. Likewise, the brambling, the male of which closely resembles the male chaffinch, is a winter visitor to this country. They move in flocks and often consort with chaffinches, but may be identified by the white patch on the back of both sexes. The siskin also belongs to this family, and as a breeding species is confined to certain parts of Scotland. It greatly favours pines and firs, making its nest of twigs and moss lined with finer roots placed at a great height and well concealed. Five or six eggs are laid, which are almost identical with those of the goldfinch.

THAT bold, handsome bird, the missel-thrush, the largest of our native thrushes, is the first to claim our attention in this chapter, for it is essentially a bird of the open fields. In appearance the missel-thrush closely resembles its near relative the song-thrush, but it is a larger and bolder bird, with a more conspicuous and heavily spotted breast. It is also sometimes confused with the fieldfare, but the latter, also a member of the thrush family, has greyish-blue upper tail coverts.

The loud song of the male is familiar throughout our countryside, and although not so varied or musical as that of the song-thrush, it has its own charm and melody. From the top branch of some tall tree the song of the missel-thrush can be heard practically throughout the year. Weather conditions do not seem to affect the songster, and even in the dull days of autumn, when most other birds are silent, the bold, robust missel-thrush continues to sing. Wind and rain are also disregarded, and in many districts the bird is known as the " Stormcock " because of its defiance of the elements.

91

At all times the missel-thrush is a shy bird, ever suspicious and distrustful of mankind. Its only friends are of its own clan, and in autumn the birds move in flocks. The harvest of hips and haws provide the missel-thrushes with a plentiful supply of food, although their menu does not consist only of berries. Insects are also eaten, and in the spring and summer the birds' dietary is almost entirely insectivorous. The young are fed on worms, flies, beetles and the like, and there can be no doubt that the birds do much good in the destruction of noxious insects.

The bird is an early nester, and one of the first signs of spring is the splitting up of the missel-thrush flocks. It is not gregarious during the breeding season, and early in the year, often in January, the male birds seek to win themselves wives. Each pair of missel-thrushes have their own territory, and no other birds, except the smaller ones, are ever tolerated within a certain range. Even magpies are attacked and driven from would-be nesting sites, and a pair of these thrushes once so relentlessly mobbed a barn owl which had taken up residence in a nearby tree that the bird decided to move to more peaceful quarters.

Although at all times the missel-thrush is a bold, courageous bird, during the nesting season it is doubly so. It tolerates nothing and nobody and never waits for an intruder to lead the attack.

92

Every time the missel-thrush is the aggressor, and no sooner does a cat or stoat appear than the male bird—which spends most of the time guarding his sitting mate—flies straight at the animal, his wings beating wildly and uttering his strong, harsh cries of protest. The hen, however, is no coward, and if she thinks her mate is getting the worst of the battle, she leaves her eggs to join him, and together they renew the attack. Many a cat has been glad to escape the fierce and savage onslaught of these outraged birds, and even such inveterate egg thieves as carrion-crows and jays are ruthlessly put to flight. I have never known the birds attack a human being, but once or twice when I have been examining their nests or photographing their young, they have come uncomfortably close.

Curiously enough, although the missel-thrush dislikes human association, it often comes near to human dwellings to nest. This may be due to the fact that being an early nester, the countryside is still without foliage and the sheltered evergreens of gardens and orchards provide comfortable nesting sites. A pair of these birds recently nested in my garden, where I have Barbary (or ring) doves flying at large. The unfortunate doves, in spite of their innocence, suffered terribly from the attacks of the thrushes, although they were quite ignorant of the latter's nest. On one occasion a dove was perched on a rustic fence where it loved to bask in the sunshine; without any warning the male thrush charged at it, knocking the dove clean off the perch.

The nest is composed of fine twigs, weed stalks, grass and moss cemented together with mud and lined with grass. It is usually placed at a height of ten or more feet, with no attempt at concealment. The four or five pale greenish-blue eggs are spotted with purple and reddish-brown, but vary a great deal in their markings, but at all times are easily recognizable. Two broods are raised in a year.

The song-thrush is also double-brood and, like its close relative the missel-thrush, often resorts to garden shrubberies and orchards to conduct its family affairs. It is a more confiding bird than the missel-thrush, and its confidence is easily won. Instances of song-thrushes coming to door-steps, window ledges, and even to human hands for food are legion, and in their friendly and confiding ways they closely resemble the robin redbreast. They are beneficial visitors to gardens, not being at all interested in the fruit or flowers, but the constant enemies of snails and slugs. Cabbage plots are favourite hunting-grounds, each bird having its own favourite anvil—usually a stone—against which it smashes the shells of the snails until the juicy contents can be pecked

MISSEL-THRUSH

SONG THRUSH

SONG THRUSH AT NEST

out. In almost every garden at least one thrush
anvil is to be found surrounded with an untidy
litter of broken shells. Worms are another
favourite delicacy of the song-thrush, and for
this fact alone it is the friend and ally of the
gardener.

Like the missel-thrush, the song-thrush is a
persistent songster, and in early spring its
melodious song is poured forth from the high
branch of some lofty, and still leafless, tree. After
the dreary days of winter the rich, loud notes of
the song-thrush are particularly welcome as
evidence of returning spring.

Song-thrushes nest early in the year, and full
clutches of eggs in February have been recorded
in mild seasons. Many of these early nests come
to grief because of their exposed position, and
because the bright blue eggs of the bird are very
obvious to egg thieves, whether they be mam-
malian, avian or human. Perhaps that is why
the song-thrush so often seeks the shelter of the
garden shrubbery, thinking that there it would
have greater protection from its natural enemies.

The nest is strongly made after the manner of
that of the missel-thrush, but is lined with wet mud.
The lining is allowed to dry thoroughly before
laying commences, and the blue eggs with the
black spots on the larger end are very conspicuous in their hard, mud cradle. The most

usual position of the nest is at a height of from four to five feet, but much variation is shown. Nests at a height of twenty feet have been found, whilst nests on the ground itself are not infrequent. Sometimes disused pots and pans are utilized as nesting sites, and I recently photographed a song-thrush's nest in a disused bucket that had been thrown into some bracken.

Female song-thrushes vary tremendously in temperament, some being close and determined sitters, only leaving their nests when forced to do so, whilst others are exceedingly nervous, and will even forsake their eggs as soon as they realize they have been located.

Both parents are devoted to their family, and when the young leave the nest—which they do three or four days before they are able to fly—the adult birds are very watchful of them. Young song-thrushes in their nest plumage are well attired for concealment, and will remain motionless in the hedgerow until you are ready to grip them with your hand. Then they scream wildly, and there is much fuss and ado with the parents, which, in their efforts to rescue their fledgling, often come perilously near to cats or vermin. A song-thrush will use the same tactics as a partridge does in order to divert one's attention from its nest or young. I once watched a song-thrush allure a stoat quite a hundred yards across

a meadow. The stoat was, I think, unaware of
the hen song-thrush brooding her eggs in a nearby
gorse bush, but the presence of this little bloodthirsty bandit of the hedgerow was not welcomed
by the male bird, and hopping just a few feet
ahead of the stoat, the wise thrush enticed the
animal to follow it the whole length of the meadow
and over the hedge into the next field. Then the
thrush returned to its sitting mate, bringing with
him a fat, juicy worm.

The song-thrush is a very clean bird, and keeps
its nest perfectly sanitary even after the young
are hatched. All excreta from the fledglings are
promptly removed, and when the young have left
their nursery there is nothing to show that the
nest has been occupied.

In our fields and gardens the blackbird is just
as popular and abundant as the song-thrush.
The two birds are closely related, but there can
be no excuse for even the merest novice to confuse
the hen blackbird with the song-thrush. True,
the hen blackbird does belie her name in that
she is not a *black bird* at all, but brownish-black
on top with a brown breast on which are darker
brown spots. The song-thrush, however, is
much lighter in general colour, and its breast is
much more of a whitish-grey, on which the spots
are blacker and more prominent. In spite of
these distinctions, however, it is surprising how

97

many country folk who have been seeing black-birds all their life confuse the two species. But there can be no mistake about the male blackbird in his rich, glossy black coat and crocus-yellow beak. He is indeed a bird of spick-and-span appearance. Blackbirds often visit gardens, where they do good work by keeping in check the snails, slugs and worms. True, it is not above helping itself to fruit, but the bird's good points out-balance its offences, and the wise gardener knows that the blackbird is his friend.

Blackbirds are among the latest of British birds to retire at night (the nocturnal birds, of course, being excepted), and long after the other members of our feathered population have gone to their sleeping places the blackbird's song can still be heard in the quiet countryside. Even when it does retire for the night it is a light sleeper and the slightest disturbance awakens it. Then there is a flutter as the alarmed bird leaves its perch, and a series of " clink, clink, clink " calls to warn its brethren of danger. I have on many occasions had cause to deplore the panic thus caused by an awakened blackbird, for such an outburst almost invariably spoils one's chances of badger-watching or other night observation. Most nocturnal animals know quite well that a black-bird's flying about at night is an unusual occur-rence, and anything unusual so far as wild

animals are concerned is closely allied to danger
—and they take no chances.

The nest of the blackbird, in outward appearance, is like the nest of the song-thrush, both being
made of grasses, but the blackbird prefers a lining
of fine grasses to one of mud. Various situations
are used for nesting, and almost anywhere that
offers seclusion will make its appeal.

The four, five or six pale greenish-blue eggs,
heavily blotched and spotted with greyish-brown,
may be looked for in late March. Two broods
are reared in a season and, in common with its
relative the song-thrush, the blackbird is very
courageous in defence of its home and family.
Any suspicious creature—no matter whether of
fur or feather—is at once challenged, the ringing
warning calls of the blackbirds bringing other
birds to their aid, until a whole battalion of
feathered allies confront the, often innocent,
intruder.

The redwing and the fieldfare—also members
of the thrush family—are winter visitors to this
country. Both are gregarious birds, and the redwing is the first of the two species to arrive.
It is about the size of a song-thrush, but may be
identified from it by the more pronounced markings and by the pale eye-stripe, as well as by its
red-tinged flank feathers, which are noticeable
beneath its wings when in flight. The male bird

is a good songster, but as it visits us only in winter we are not privileged to hear its vocal abilities. While it sojourns here the redwing haunts the open fields, usually in flocks, but with the return of spring it leaves us for its Norwegian home, where it conducts its family affairs and where the male bird's song is heard at its best.

The fieldfare is larger than the redwing and is sometimes mistaken for the missel-thrush, from which, however, it may be identified by its slate grey head and back and conspicuous black tail. In April fieldfares leave this country for northern Europe.

The ring-ouzel, or mountain blackbird, as it is often called, is a member of this family and a summer visitor to this country, but it is a bird of the mountains and moors.

THE BUNTINGS

THE buntings are birds that haunt various types of country—the fields, the commons and heathland, and even the moors and marshes, but it is to our fields that three of the four species represented in our islands primarily belong. They are the yellow-bunting (or yellow-hammer), the cirl-bunting and the corn-bunting.

The yellow-bunting is the most common of its tribe, and is so called because of the richness of its yellow markings. The female is less brightly coloured than her mate, although her markings are the same as his but less conspicuous.

The nest is usually built in a hedge among tangled herbage but sometimes a bush is used. On the ground itself is not an unusual site, but my field records show an increasing tendency for yellow-buntings to nest at a greater height, and during the breeding season of 1937, out of the eight yellow-buntings' nests discovered five were more than six feet above ground and the remaining three above four feet. It is a neatly made nest of roots and grasses lined with hair and is usually well hidden. Both birds assist in the building of the nest and the incubation. When off the nest the male bird seldom leaves the vicinity of its home and has his own favourite perches from which to act as sentinel. He has a song which has been likened to " A little bit of bread and no che-e-se ", and whilst the performance is far from being musical, it is pleasant.

The four or five eggs are very distinctive and very peculiarly marked. The ground surface is a dirty-white with a purplish tint, on which are streaks and marks of a purplish colour. The eggs look as if they had been scribbled on with purple ink, which subsequently had " run ". It is to its peculiarly marked eggs that the yellow-bunting owes its local name of " scribbling lark ". Two broods are raised in a season and nests and eggs in August are not unusual.

The cirl-bunting is far less common than the yellow-bunting, but each species rather closely resembles the other unless seen within close range. This is especially true of the female birds of both species, the main distinguishing feature being the olive-green rump of the cirl-bunting, in contrast to the yellowish-brown rump of its relative. The male cirl-bunting, however, has a black bib and black eye-stripe to distinguish him. These differences, however, although easily recognizable when the birds are seen at close quarters, are none too evident from a distance, and this, I think, is partly responsible for the supposed

102

rarity of the cirl-bunting. I must confess that I have myself often been surprised when bringing field-glasses to bear on a supposed flock of yellow-buntings to find among them several cirl-buntings. But for the help of my field-glasses these latter would not have been recognized.

The cirl-bunting is a late nester, and it is seldom that eggs are laid before May. The nest is similar to that of the yellow-bunting, as also are the eggs, except that the latter show fewer but heavier markings. In their family affairs the sexes are very devoted to each other, but they are more nervous than yellow-buntings and will readily leave their nests and eggs if interfered with. The bird's range is mainly confined to the southern and western parts of England and Wales.

The corn-bunting is the largest of its clan and, compared with the two species we have discussed in this chapter, is a plain, sombre bird. It is a great lover of cultivated fields, especially corn-fields, from which it gets its name.

The nest is a rather large one for the size of the bird and is loosely made of grasses and roots. It is usually placed on or near the ground and well hidden in growing herbage. The four or five eggs are like those of other buntings, but show great variation in the markings.

A peculiar trait in the character of corn-buntings is that, in some districts, the male birds are polygamous, each male having two, three or even four mates, whilst in other districts monogamy is the prevailing practice. To explain this variation in habit is, at the moment, more than I care to attempt, but it is probable that naturalists and observers who are working on this subject will soon be able to give a satisfactory explanation. I rather incline to the theory, however, that polygamy is only indulged in in those districts where, for some reason or other, there happens to be an abundance of hen birds.

The reed-bunting and the snow-bunting are two other members of this family, but they are not birds of the fields.

THE curlew is a difficult bird to classify according to the type of country it haunts, for it is just as much a bird of the marshes and commons as it is of the fields; in the winter it is not an infrequent visitor to our sea-shores.

I have, however, decided to place it among the birds of our fields, as it is in the wild, open pastures that I have had the opportunity of studying the behaviour and habits of the curlew.

I have always found the curlew, in spite of its wary nature, an interesting subject to study, and have spent many hours in a " hide " with field-glasses and camera watching and recording the curlew's daily routine. The bird gets its name from its call-note—a wild, melancholy sort of cry which is uttered frequently both when the bird is in flight and when on the ground. But in addition to the familiar call-note of " cur-lew, cur-lew ", the bird can produce many other equally melancholy and wailing cries, many of which are heard at night, for the curlew is a bird that is often active in the dusk. In the stillness of the night and in the solitude of a large, open field, the shrill calls of the curlews produce an eerie atmosphere, intensified by the noise of their wildly beating wings.

There is, however, at least one tune in the curlew's vocabulary which is pleasant, if not musical, and that is the bird's rippling love-song, so familiar to those folk who have been privileged to visit the nesting-ground of curlews.

Curlews may be recognized when on the ground by their long legs, speckled plumage and long, curved beak. In flight their frequently uttered call-note is an unfailing guide to their identification, and when they rise from the ground or alighting, their extended wings reveal their white rump.

At no time of the year is the curlew more watchful and wary than during the breeding season. The nest, or to be more correct, the depression in which the eggs are laid (for nothing in the nature of a nest is attempted), is in the open, and although not cleverly concealed, is most difficult to find. The curlew practices camouflage, and I have many a time passed within a few inches of the nest, wherein lay four eggs fully exposed, without my knowing it. A few dead leaves and some grass as a lining for the depression is all the curlew does by way of nest-making.

To locate the nest is, as I have already said, difficult, and even when you see the bird leave

YOUNG CURLEWS

it, it is not easy to find the place from which she actually left. The open fields have few places as " landmarks ", and many nests which have been discovered by mere chance have been looked for in vain the second time.

The eggs of the curlew, usually four, are olive-green in ground colour, blotched and spotted with brown and grey. Much variation is shown both in the ground colour and in the markings, but whatever their appearance they so closely resemble their surroundings as to elude the eye.

The eggs are pear-shaped and arranged with the pointed ends pointing inwards. No matter how often the position of the eggs be changed, the curlew, immediately it reaches home, notices the change and rearranges her treasures again. This is a practice with one or two other birds besides the curlew, and many reasons have been advanced for such persistent behaviour; the most widely accepted theory being that in the position favoured by the bird the eggs are more easily brooded. Whilst this may be true in relation to certain species of birds, especially those birds which lay rather large eggs for their size, it cannot be seriously considered in relation to all birds which indulge in the habit.

Brooding often is, for the curlews, an irksome task, as nesting in the open means that the sitting bird is fully exposed to all weather. I have often seen brooding curlews covering their eggs in a deluge of rain with nothing more than a few blades of grass to shelter them. I have also seen them in the scorching sun of a hot summer's day when the heat must have been almost unbearable. Not a particle of shade protects the birds as they patiently incubate, with beak wide open, panting under the distress of the sun.

Fortunately, both sexes share the period of incubation, and are so much alike in plumage that to distinguish between them is almost impossible. I have often watched the " change over " from the duty of incubating, and the sitting bird is always obviously pleased to be relieved of its duties.

Baby curlews are charming little creatures, covered with a fluff of brownish-grey streaked with black, and are active within about an hour after hatching. They are not easily found, since their colouring harmonizes so perfectly with their environment. They also have the instinct, common to most young ground birds, to squat motionless when alarmed. They do not stand in great fear of mankind, and when once captured seem to reconcile themselves to the situation. I have had baby curlews stand on my hand quite undisturbed, and they have a remarkable habit of remaining where they are placed. Many photographs have been taken of young curlews deliberately placed on a stone or fence or in one's hand without any of the pains and problems so well known to the wild bird photographer.

The parents show great courage in defence of their little ones, but often unconsciously act indiscreetly in giving forth their angry, shrill cries when an intruder appears, thus betraying the whereabouts of their fledglings. Actually, the curlew's idea is to warn the youngsters, but to the experienced bird-lover it is a never-failing intimation that somewhere nearby are fluffy brown chicks.

The curlew is often mistaken for its near relative the whimbrel, which it greatly resembles, but the whimbrel is much the smaller of the two. The latter's chief breeding range is in the Shetlands, and the bird will be dealt with more fully elsewhere.

The green plover, lapwing or pee-wit, to give it its alternative names, is the bird which next claims our attention, and this bird, like the curlew, has a wide range of territory as its haunts. I include it in this chapter because plovers are such familiar birds on arable land, and as in their erratic flight they wheel over our pastures.

If I were asked to say which of the two birds, the curlew or the green plover, has the more pathetic, melancholy calls, I confess I could not make up my mind. The cry of the plover is certainly mournful, but the bird has the ability to vary its call-notes, and some are less of a wail than others; the bird's early spring calls are the most musical of its vocabulary. I think the different calls of the plover, as is the case with most other birds, are expressive of inward feelings; some are cries of alarm or fear, other cries being merely of a " conversational " nature, while the love-calls are the most pleasant of all and express pleasure and happiness. Some of our small birds of the fields act similarly, and the chaffinch's " pink, pink's " as he perches on the side of the mossy home in which his wife is sitting, is far different to the wild, excited "pink, pink's " which he utters when danger threatens his home. What, for instance, is more pleasant to listen to than the call of the blackbird as he arrives at his nest with food, and what is more sharp and metallic than the warning notes of this black-coated gentleman?

Plovers are easily recognized by their head-crests, as no other British bird possesses any similar head-plumes, but their plumage is also distinctive, for their olive-green backs, white breast and dark neck-band are not found in any other of our birds.

Their black, rounded wings and their white breasts are very prominent when the birds are in flight, and a flock of plovers flying helter-skelter over our fields is one of the most familiar sights of our countryside in autumn and winter. They love the open spaces, where there is nothing to impede their flight and progress. Like the curlew, the plover is often heard at night, when its long drawn-out " pee-weet " is as mournful and foreboding as the calls of the curlew.

Nesting begins in April, when the flocks separate and the wedded pairs settle down in the breeding quarters. The hen bird is particular in her choice of a nesting site, and fields, commons, marshes and hilltops are visited. No nest is made, the eggs being laid in a slight depression in growing herbage or grass. The site is usually exposed and some distance from hedges, trees or other cover, which is perhaps more by design than accident, for ground-nesting birds have many enemies whose homes are in the hedgerow. The hedgehog regards eggs as a delicacy, and stoats and weasels are also to be feared both as regards their liking for eggs and later on for the chicks.

A few weed stalks and grasses are used as a lining for the selected nesting site, but there is no attempt at nest-building. There is usually some confusion before the site is actually decided upon, the hen bird being most difficult to please. Anxious to help his wife, the male bird does a great deal of fussing about, scratching here and there, suggesting first one place and then another

111

and even carrying materials in his anxiety at home-making. More often than not, however, the hen bird ignores all his suggestions, and eventually selects an entirely different site altogether. But this does not weaken the male bird's devotion and, as all good husbands should do, he commences to provide the few stalks and stems necessary to complete the home.

The four greenish-brown eggs are blotched with black and grey and blend perfectly with their surroundings. They are not easy to find, and the birds never give any clue as to the whereabouts of their nest. When the hen leaves her eggs she slips off them quickly and runs a few feet pretending her unconcern. Both birds resort to various tactics in order to divert one's attention from their nest, none of which is more frequently employed than the broken-wing trick. If the hen bird is sitting her mate will indulge in all sorts of aerial displays, continually swooping to within a few inches of an intruder's head.

Plovers' eggs are often sold in shops, for they are exceedingly tasty, but the law forbids it. They are pear-shaped, the points being arranged inwards when in the nest.

The young are covered in a fluffy, brown down streaked with black and grey, and are very difficult to find when they squat among the herbage. Within a few hours of hatching the young are able to run quite strongly, and are a pretty sight to watch as they follow their parents in search of food.

A bird of similar habits to the green plover, or lapwing, and haunting similar country, is the golden plover. The speckled plumage of this bird is quite different to that of any other British bird of a like size.

The golden plover nests on the ground in similar situations to those occupied by the green plover, the four eggs being of a yellowish-buff colour with pronounced brownish-grey markings. The fluffy young also have the advantage of protective coloration. The bird breeds abundantly in Scotland and also in certain parts of Ireland, but in England it is confined as a breeding species to the north and north-western districts.

In winter flocks of golden plover haunt grass-land. They are swift flyers and when on the wing or on the ground are usually recognizable by their clear, liquid whistle call-notes, by which they are known in many districts as " Whistlers ".

Also on the British list is the Kentish plover —a summer visitor to Britain and confined mainly to Kent; the ringed plover, which is definitely a bird of the sea-shore, and one or two other species which are such rare visitors as not to merit mention here.

UNFORTUNATELY, the landrail, or corn-crake, is getting rare in many parts of this country, although actually it was never really abundant anywhere. It is a migrant and arrives here usually in May.

Owing to its elusive habits it is more often heard than seen, and in spite of the fact that the landrail calls almost continuously throughout the hours of daylight and often well on into the night, the bird is not easily located. It is so very difficult to trace the sound of the landrail's harsh, creaking call-notes; there seems to be a ven-triloquial quality in its voice, so that it appears to come from here, there and anywhere.

Landrails are almost as nocturnal as they are diurnal, and in the summer months the birds may be heard calling at any hour throughout the night. Even when one succeeds in tracking down the bird to within a certain area, it is difficult actually to discover it and still more difficult to flush it into flight. The fact that the landrail frequents fields of growing corn, from the depths of which its " crake, crake "

114

GOLDEN PLOVER

CORNCRAKE ON NEST

calls come, makes it all the more difficult to find the bird.

Single-handed it is almost impossible, and I have tried and failed hundreds of times. A dog I once had, however, was very successful in flushing landrails and was a great help to me in my field work. That dog was also a wonderful aid in locating such birds as nightjars, sitting curlews and lapwings, no doubt owing to his acute sense of smell.

When one person, single-handed, attempts to flush a landrail, the bird naturally slips away ahead of the searcher and never reveals itself unless by some mistake it comes out into the open. The best way to stalk the bird is for four (or more) searchers to start from different angles and carefully close in upon the bird. But the bird is adept at concealing itself, and even when forced to take to its wings it seldom rises more than two feet above ground. The flight is strong and swift, but gives the impression that the bird is at great disadvantage. It does not fly far before resettling. Actually, however, the landrail must be able and efficient on the wing, for being a migrant it has to fly long distances. Once the bird has reached these shores, however, it gives its wings all the rest it possibly can, and except when flushed, a landrail in flight is an unusual sight.

The landrail nests in fields of growing hay more often than anywhere else, although nests in corn-fields are not uncommon; hay, however, being of thicker growth, provides the bird with better cover and is freer from rats and mice than are corn-fields.

The nest consists of grasses and leaves roughly interwoven and placed in a shallow depression in the ground. The pale, buff-coloured eggs, which number from eight to ten, are spotted and blotched with mauve and reddish-brown.

The modern methods of farming are largely responsible for the decrease in the numbers of landrails. In earlier days when scythes were used, the sitting birds could escape, but the reaping-machines of to-day spare neither the sitting birds nor the eggs, and hundreds of fledglings must also meet their death this way. When the first nests have been destroyed, I believe the bird makes a second attempt, for nests and eggs in August are not unusual. Too often, however, for these later nests the landrail chooses the fields of growing corn, only to again meet with disaster when the harvest comes.

The chicks are covered with a black down and rather like young moorhens in appearance. Within about an hour after hatching they are able to run about and follow their parents. Even when but a few days old the chicks are able to run at a tremendous speed, and soon learn to dart here and there after insects, of which the crane-fly or " Daddy-long-legs " is a great favourite.

In colour the landrail is yellowish-brown above, streaked with black, and has chestnut coloured wings. When flushed into flight the bird rises clumsily with legs dangling, and cannot be mistaken for any other British bird, for although from a distance it superficially resembles the partridge, the landrail may be distinguished by its smaller size.

THE SHORT-EARED OWL

ALTHOUGH the short-eared owl in appearance resembles the owl tribe in general, there are two important characteristics in which it differs. Firstly, it is not a bird of the trees and woodland, and secondly, it moves about by day as well as by night.

It is best known in this country as a winter visitor, although many instances of the bird breeding here have been authentically recorded, and there is every evidence that such instances are on the increase.

The bird's facial characteristics—round face and large eyes—would at once identify it as a member of the owl family, but the name " short-eared " is not so appropriate. The name comes from two tufts of feathers, one of which grows on either side of the bird's head, but these are so inconspicuous as to be almost unnoticeable unless the bird is excited. Under excitement the ear-tufts are raised and then become noticeable, but in the fields and wide open spaces which the short-eared owl frequents, the ear-tufts are not visible to the casual observer. In the case of the long-eared owl [1] the head appendages are more prominent, but in neither species have they anything to do with the bird's organs of hearing.

Short-eared owls generally reach these shores in small parties, but the companies soon break up, and solitary birds are usual, except during the nesting season. The behaviour of the short-eared owl is, to say the least, irregular, and in some years certain districts are favoured with several nesting birds, whilst another year those same districts cannot boast one nest.

It is evident that the abundance, or otherwise, of food determines to a great extent the owl's movements, and in those districts where voles and mice are plentiful the birds often remain to breed. A friend of mine recently told me that some years ago he discovered four short-eared owls' nests in the heather and coarse grass of an uncultivated meadow which was less than an acre of ground. Their presence was probably due to the number of field voles which that year almost constituted a plague in that district, for the following year, when the plague had abated, only one pair of short-eared owls nested in the vicinity.

The short-eared owl always nests on the ground in the open with a tuft of heather, grass or bracken to conceal her eggs. No nest is made, although at times a few sticks are collected as a

[1] See *At Home in the Woods.*

lining for the slight depression in which the white eggs are laid. The number of eggs varies considerably, but from four to eight are the usual number. An abundance of food would seem also to have its effect on the number of eggs, for when food is plentiful nests are more numerous and larger clutches of eggs are usual.

The eggs are laid on alternate days and incubation commences with the laying of the first egg, so that by the time the last egg has hatched out the earliest hatched youngster is a fortnight or more old.

As these words leave my pen my memory takes me back some years ago, when a very dear friend (he has since been called to the homeland) and myself set out to find a short-eared owl's nest which a gamekeeper told us he was sure was " somewhere on the downs ". The downs were some fifty or sixty acres, through which flowed two small streams—one on the eastern and one on the western side. We decided to keep together and make the search jointly. After two hours' heavy walking over heather and through gorse, we saw an owl approaching. Its wing-beats were deliberate and steady, the wings appearing long and narrow. As the owl came nearer, it appeared to be losing its strength, and gave us the impression of a wounded bird unable to fly to its haven, yet trying to escape from danger. Suddenly it twisted, turned somersaults, rose higher into the air again and then swooped. Minutes passed and it did not take wing again, so we wended our way to where it had dropped. Before we reached the bird we could see it through field-glasses standing motionless on the ground, its large eyes focused upon us, but it was not until we were within arm's reach that it rose into the air, its wings clapping like pistol shots, while it repeatedly barked like a dog. The bird's behaviour was evidently a ruse to attract our attention, and it was probable that we were close to its sitting mate. After a great deal of screaming and barking another short-eared owl appeared from the direction in which we had come.

It seemed probable that the nest was on the eastern side—the side from which we had set out —but our chances of finding it would be considerably increased when the hen bird was in the nest, so we decided to conceal ourselves for a while in a disused building from which we could keep observation on the surrounding territory.

Eventually both owls alighted quite near the spot which we had left, and after giving the birds time to compose themselves we set out once again towards the eastern stream. Suddenly, on looking back, we saw two owls rise into the air from the western stream and leisurely make their way towards us. The position was getting complicated. Were these the same two owls we had previously seen, or were there two pairs in the area? Were they, indeed, short-eared owls? With the aid of field-glasses, coupled with the fact that the birds had been resting on the ground and were flying abroad in the daylight (habits not usually met with in other owls), we satisfied ourselves that this pair, too, were of the short-eared variety.

One of our difficulties, however, was soon solved, for suddenly there appeared, as if created by some magic wand, a third long-eared owl! Our search was proving exciting, for we were now satisfied that two pairs existed.

We had previously marked by the presence of a large stone the area in which we believed the owls had their nest, and were particularly keen to reach the spot in case the hen bird decided to leave it in order to investigate the heated argument which was now taking place in mid-air among three owls. The presence of the other two birds engaged the attentions of the third, whose nest we sought, to his utter disregard for our presence until we were within a few feet of our landmark. Then pandemonium broke out; swooping perilously near our faces and doing all sorts of tricks in order to entice us from the spot, he barked like an infuriated terrier. But we were determined not to be deceived a second time by his antics, and

122

SHORT-EARED OWL ON NEST

SHORT-EARED OWL APPROACHING NEST

so a thorough search began. We knew by the male bird's behaviour that we were in the danger zone, but to locate the actual site of the nest proved more difficult than we had imagined.

Bracken, tussocky grass and herbage were all searched until finally, almost on the point of deferring the search until the next day, we were rewarded by finding three owl castings ("castings" or " pellets " are little balls of indigestible food which owls disgorge, for they swallow their food whole [1]), and knew that the object of our search was close at hand. Then a movement beneath a low gorse bush attracted our attention, and there two glaring yellow eyes met ours. Except for a few blades of grass nothing hid the owl, she had been exposed to our view all the time, and we had probably looked at her again and again without actually having " seen " her. Her protective coloration was excellent.

Her wings were wide-spread, which indicated that she was covering owlets, and we yielded to the temptation to flush her from the nest. Meanwhile her mate had continued his loud barking protests overhead, and when the hen joined him his courage increased. It looked as if we might be called upon at any moment to a hand-battle with his beak and talons, but we managed to examine the two owlets which, with four eggs, were the

[1] *At Home in the Woods*, Ch. VII.

treasures that the devoted mother had been covering, and then went quickly home. Other duties prevented our attempting to locate the nest of the second pair of short-eared owls on the western side of the downs, but it was to this particular pair of birds that the gamekeeper referred who first put us wise to the presence of the owls.

The eggs of the short-eared owl are, as I have already stated, laid on alternate days, and the young are hatched accordingly. When each becomes strong enough it leaves the nest and wanders away into the surrounding cover, where the parents visit it regularly. By the time the whole family has separated the parents have a very busy time visiting each youngster in turn and finding sufficient food to satisfy their large appetites.

At a very early age the owlets are able to use their talons to good purpose in attack or defence, and a stout pair of leather gloves is advisable when handling them.

Because of its habit of hunting by day, one might well expect the short-eared owl to take heavy toll of bird-life, but my observation does not confirm this. Over a period of six or seven years I have examined many scores of castings from these birds, and in very few instances only have I found traces of birds. Voles seem to be the short-eared owl's mainstay, but field mice,

124

shrews and rats are included in its menu. There can be no question of the economic value of this species to agriculturists, and it is to be hoped that everything possible will be done to encourage migrating birds to nest here.

THE WAGTAILS

WAGTAILS are among the most interesting of our small birds. They inhabit various types of country, and are as much at home by the waterside as in the fields. One might also class them as birds of the garden, for few indeed are the garden paths or lawns which do not boast some members of the wagtail family. The birds —more especially the pied wagtail—also love the commons and the hillsides, and often frequent orchards and tumbled buildings. They seem at home almost anywhere except in the woods. One occasionally finds a pair on the fringe of a small coppice, but not often, for trees hold no attraction for wagtails.

They often visit farmyards, especially in winter months, when they are also regular visitors to feeding-tables. Insects, in season, form the mainstay of their dietary, and it is on this food that the young are reared. They often alight on the backs of grazing cattle to catch the insects which greatly worry the animals during the summer. All the wagtails are alike in many characteristics, their flight being of an undulating nature and usually accompanied by a series of call-notes. They never *hop* over the ground, but progress by walking or running—more often the latter, for all the wagtails are lively and almost constantly on the move. The tail is for ever a-wagging, from which the birds have very appropriately been named. They are extraordinarily clever at catching insects, and often perform some amazing aerial feats when insect-hunting in mid-air. Except when searching trees and bushes for insect-fare, the wagtails are more often to be found on the ground than anywhere else, as they are more at home walking than perching. I once kept a pet pied wagtail which seldom perched at all, even preferring to sleep in the undergrowth of the aviary to which he retired each night. When asleep, he more often squatted on the ground than stood on his legs, and made himself a cosy retreat in the grass in a sheltered corner of the aviary. When spring came round this bachelor wagtail constructed a nest in a slight depression (which I believe he made himself) adjoining his sleeping chamber, but unfortunately, never succeeded in attracting a mate. But a funny thing happened; a pair of long-tailed field mice appropriated the nest, roofed it over, added a few feathers, and were soon the proud parents of four baby mice; even the elegant long-tailed field mice are not desirable visitors in an aviary, how-

ever, and I was obliged to destroy the litter.
But the wagtail did not object to his visitors, and
for many nights he occupied his own sleeping
chamber, whilst less than six inches away the
field mice occupied theirs. Because of the
tremendous waste of food for which the mice
were responsible (the amount they actually *ate*
was almost negligible) I was eventually obliged
to trap them.

The following spring my pet wagtail mated
and nested in the garden, using an artificial
nesting-box that had been fixed on a trellis fence.
Four fledglings were reared, and the whole family
have remained until this day within the precincts
of the homestead, but the old bird has never
since returned to his aviary.

I think the pied wagtail—locally known as the
" dish-washer "—is the most common and widely
distributed member of its genus. The reason for
this latter name has been variously explained,
but if, as has been suggested, it is because of the
bird's association with water, the title is certainly
unjustified. True, some of the pied wagtails enjoy
paddling about in shallow pools and even haunt
the banks of rivers and streams, but thousands of
these birds live inland many miles from any
watering place. The absence of water certainly
does not inconvenience the bird, and it is just as
much at home among the rocks and boulders of

the hillside as it is in the well-watered valley.

The pied wagtail may be recognized by its dark back and rump, and may be distinguished from its Continental relative, the white wagtail, by its darker general appearance and its less conspicuous black throat and chest-patch. There is a strong resemblance, however, between the two birds, so strong a resemblance that many naturalists still doubt if they are separate species.

The male pied wagtail has a very amusing courting display when attempting to win the attentions of some female. All sorts of short flights are indulged in as well as much strutting, jumping, bowing and similar antics. The tail plays an important part in these courting displays and is kept almost continuously bobbing up and down.

The nest is made of hay, grass stalks and roots with a lining of feathers, wool and hair. It is usually placed on a firm foundation such as a stone, ledge or other support and under cover. A crevice in a hedge or wall is often utilized, whilst suitable positions in quarries, old buildings, thatched roofs and rocky slopes are also occupied. The four to six eggs have a speckled appearance, the ground colour being greyish-white, sometimes inclining to a purplish hue. Eggs are not often laid until the first week in April, but it is usual for two broods to be raised in a season.

The pied wagtail readily tenants artificial nesting-boxes if they are provided in secluded and sheltered positions. Among growing ivy is as good a position as anywhere, the boxes being of the open-fronted type—a style which also appeals to robins. The wagtails have a tendency to return to the same nesting site on successive years, and young reared in an artificial receptacle show a marked inclination for similar accommodation for their own nests the following year.

A friend of mine who some years ago provided a nesting-box for a pair of wagtails, in which four young were reared, had three boxes occupied the following spring. Some of the young were ringed, and it was the offspring that returned the following year. Subsequently he learned that the hen birds returned (not the males) to nest in the vicinity of their old home, and it looks as if the wagtail population in my friend's grounds will soon reach overcrowding conditions.

The pied wagtail is often victimized by the cuckoo irrespective of the situation of the nest. In the spring of 1937 I located a wagtail's nest between two large stones in a quarry, and was erecting a hide from which to photograph it when I noticed a cuckoo glide towards the site and for a second or two halt on quivering wings as if to examine the nest. Continued observation revealed that the cuckoo was definitely interested,

PIED WAGTAIL AT NEST

and probably intended to impose upon this pair of wagtails the duties of hatching her egg and rearing the young. This particular case was of rather unusual interest to me because of the fact that the crevice in which the nest was situated did not appear to be large enough to admit the cuckoo. If there were any foundation for the old theory that the cuckoo lays her egg on the ground and then carries it in her beak to the selected nest, it would certainly be to her advantage to do so in this instance. But nothing of the kind happened, and some days afterwards I saw the cuckoo alight at the site, pick up one of the wagtail's eggs, shuffle her way backwards on to the nest, and lay her egg.

Pied wagtails are abundant throughout the year, but migration takes place, and the birds that nest here are not the same birds that winter with us. The birds that nest here fly south in the autumn and other migrants take their place.

The white wagtail, as I have already mentioned, closely resembles the pied wagtail, and the most outstanding difference in plumage is the white wagtail's prominent black bib. It is much rarer than its pied relative, and although once considered a bird of passage only, is now rightly regarded as one of our breeding species. Nesting habits are very similar to those of the pied wagtail and the eggs are also like the latter bird's, but some show tendency to a more bluish-green ground colour. The two specimens have inter-bred, but the white wagtail is slightly the smaller of the two.

The grey wagtail is more fond of pools and running water than any other of its tribe, although the yellow wagtail, with which the grey is often confused, shows a similar inclination for marsh-land. The name, grey wagtail, is rather confusing, for the bird's yellow breast is more noticeable than its grey upper parts. However, the yellow of this bird's plumage is less prominent than the pure yellow under-surface of the yellow wagtail. When the two species are seen together the dis-tinction is very evident, but it is less so to the uninitiated when the birds are viewed separately.

The yellow flanks and tail coverts of the grey wagtail are very conspicuous in flight.

Nesting situations are almost identical with those occupied by the pied wagtail, and any secure and cosy cavity is utilized. The bird prefers, however, to nest in the vicinity of running water, and a field through which a stream flows is an ideal situation. An overhanging stone provides excellent cover for the grey wagtail's nest, which is composed of fine roots, grass and moss and lined with hair; feathers are seldom used by the grey wagtail.

The four to six eggs are creamy-white, thickly

speckled with purplish-brown; the markings vary considerably and occasionally black streaks and freckles occur. Two broods are often raised in a season, the first in April and the second in June, but the rule is variable, and I think a second brood depends on whether or not the first was reared fairly early in the season. If, for example, the first family were delayed until May, the chances are that no second brood would be attempted.

The grey wagtail is nowhere abundant although it may be found practically throughout Britain. Because of its solitary nature and its habit of moving about singly or in pairs, it often passes unnoticed. Occasionally five or six may be seen in company, but these, I believe, are usually a family party.

The most elegant and graceful of all the wagtails is the yellow wagtail, a summer visitor which arrives here in March or April. The early haunts of the yellow wagtails are the damp and marshy meadows where, owing to the heavy rains of winter and early spring, they find ample insect fare. These newly-arrived visitors also frequent farmyards, where the dung heaps invariably yield some dainty and favourite items of their insectivorous menu.

The yellow wagtail is most appropriately named, the bird's under-parts and prominent eye-stripe being of the pure buttercup yellow, the back is greenish-yellow, the female being more subdued in colour than her mate. In winter, both sexes are less brightly coloured.

The nest of this species is generally placed on the ground, cleverly concealed in growing grass or herbage. It is an open cup-shaped structure composed of the materials common to the wag-tail tribe, but is a more loosely-made affair; a lining is always added but the materials vary; sometimes feathers are utilized and sometimes they are not. There is always a quantity of horse-hair, but the presence of feathers would seem to be determined by the type of country inhabited, for I have noticed that feathers are seldom used in those nests built near running water, whilst in nests in pasture lands and growing corn crops they are invariably present.

Occasionally yellow wagtails nest in small colonies, due, I think, to the presence of suitable nesting sites rather than to their gregarious nature during the breeding season. When nests are found in close proximity they are usually placed in thick, coarse grass such as grows on croftlands or commons. I do not think the different pairs of birds quarrel without justification, but there is little friendship among them. Each wedded couple seems to go their own way quite oblivious of their next-door neighbours. The fledglings when they leave the nest are also indifferent to the children next door, yet with the return of autumn the families congregate to make arrangements for their journey to warmer climes.

Lastly comes the blue-headed wagtail, which is a rare but regular visitor to this country and a lover of the open fields. It may be distinguished from the yellow wagtail by its bluish-grey head and its white eye-stripe. As a breeding species it is rare in Britain. Its nesting habits are almost identical with those of the yellow wagtail, and as the females of the two species so closely resemble each other, it is exceedingly difficult to decide to which species a nest belongs without seeing the male birds. The eggs of the two species are also so much alike as to be of no help whatever in their identification and the fledglings are equally indistinguishable.

OTHER BIRDS OF THE FIELDS

I DO not know who first called the hedge accentor (commonly known as hedge-sparrow) that " little drab bird of the bushes ", but the description is admirably chosen. It certainly is a drab little bird, and from a distance resembles the hen house-sparrow which is why, perhaps, the bird has come to be called by the name of hedge-sparrow. Actually, however, it is not even remotely related to the sparrow family, and its slender beak and bluish-grey head are sufficient to distinguish it.

The song of the hedge accentor is not unlike that of the robin, but it is inclined to be more flat and with fewer variations. The bird is widely distributed throughout the country except in the extreme northern regions of Scotland.

In spite of its drab attire the hedge accentor is an interesting bird to study, very lively and cheery and almost constantly uttering its little song. Even when most other birds are silent, the hedge accentor continues its musical performance. It is among the early nesters, and its open cup-shaped nest, composed of fine twigs, roots and moss, closely lined with hair, is often to be found

136

in March. The hedge accentor shares with the song-thrush and our other early nesting birds the difficulty of finding secluded nesting sites early in spring and, because of this, the bird often visits garden shrubberies and evergreens, there to construct its early home. Later nests, however, are situated farther afield, the bird being particularly fond of a gorse bush. Nesting positions, however, vary greatly, and the situation chosen may be anywhere from one foot to six feet above ground. The nest itself is cleverly made and usually well concealed. There is an inclination for the birds to return year after year to the same nesting sites, and I believe they pair for life. A certain gorse bush in a country lane along which I often wander was the site of a hedge accentor's nest for five years in succession. I cannot say definitely that the same pair of birds were the occupiers, but in many cases that have come to my notice of birds wearing rings, the same pairs occupy the same sites in succeeding years.

The beautiful greenish-blue eggs of the hedge accentor are generally devoid of gloss and unspotted. There may be four, five, or six in number, and because of their bright colour are easily seen by jays and magpies, especially if, as in the case of early nests, there is little foliage to conceal them. Two or three broods are raised in a year, and the hedge accentor's nest is often the first and the last to be found.

My field notes prove that in my own experience the hedge accentor is the most frequently victimized by the cuckoo of any British bird.

Although the hedge accentor visits gardens and to a great extent becomes friendly, it seldom uses artificial nesting receptacles of any description. I have often provided various types of nesting-boxes for birds, but none has ever been tenanted by the hedge accentor. Once, however, a pair nested in a tin hat (worn by a soldier during the Great War) that had been left in a clump of pampas grass. Unfortunately a cat discovered the young just before they were old enough to leave the nest and killed them all. Whether the parents would have nested there again I do not know, for I removed the old relic of those awful years to prevent a similar tragedy happening to any other birds which chanced to build there.

One of our earliest summer visitors is the wheatear, and seldom does March pass before some of these interesting birds are with us. The male bird is of smart appearance, with his white forehead and under parts, slate-grey back with a black and white tail that shows up very prominently as the bird flies from place to place.

Although the wheatear frequents different types of country, it is a regular visitor to fields

WHEATEAR AT NESTING PLACE

and commons. It is also a lover of the moors and marshes, but wherever it makes its home it at once settles down and seldom wanders far until it leaves the country for its winter home.

The wheatear is very fond of old buildings, stone walls, or even piles of stones that have been carted into the corners of fields. The hen bird is not so brightly or distinctively attired as her mate, being browner, but she possesses the prominent white upper tail coverts.

It is in holes in walls or hedges, and frequently down a rabbit-hole, that the wheatear constructs its rather untidy and clumsy nest, the outer walls of which are constructed of roots, stems and grass, a cosy lining of hair, wool and feathers being added. Because of its concealed position the nest is very difficult to find, and the hen bird is very careful not to betray its whereabouts. It is a common practice of wheatears to run to a hole or crevice for shelter or when pursued, but never does a hen bird seek the shelter of her nesting burrow. I have even known an incubating hen slip from her eggs when discovered and move farther inwards rather than emerge into view.

The nest, however, is more easily located when the young arrive, for they are continually calling for food, and when old enough are often seen, with their beaks wide open, at the entrance to their nesting hole, waiting for food. The five or six eggs of the wheatear are pale blue in colour, and may be first looked for in April. Two broods are sometimes reared in a year, but the rule is variable.

Although a great lover of the heaths and commons, the stonechat is a regular inhabitant of our fields, where the male bird, with his black throat and head, and his black-and-white back and bright orange-red breast, makes himself prominent. The hen bird is less conspicuously attired, although her plumage is patterned almost exactly like her mate's. The male stonechat is not easily overlooked because of his fondness for perching in exposed places. The tallest branch of a gorse bush is always chosen in preference to a lower one, and from this prominent perch the bird calls loudly and clearly " u-tec, u-tec, u-tec ", flicking his tail the while.

Stonechats are resident birds throughout the British Isles, but there is also evidence of migration. There is an inclination for the birds to visit coastal districts after the breeding season, but a few of them, probably the older birds, remain in the fields and heathlands throughout the year.

In the winter, however, the stonechat is but a ghost of its former self. The male bird loses the brilliance of his chestnut-red breast and the black-

and-white of its back also become less distinctive, and he more closely resembles his mate. His demeanour, too, is different, for he is no longer the indignant assertive and important bird which so loudly proclaimed his authority in the summer months.

Early in March the stonechat returns to its breeding haunts, and the males again assume their bright attire and dignity. Whether the birds pair for life I cannot say; at times it looks as if they do, but certain it is that during their wedded period they are very devoted to one another.

Each pair of birds keep strictly to their own territory — there is no neighbourliness among stonechats. Members of their own tribe are not respected any more than birds of another clan. It does not take the male stonechat long to adopt a pugnacious attitude towards birds much bigger than himself.

The nest is a rough structure of roots and grass lined with finer grass, hair and sometimes feathers. The position of the nest is usually low down, where it is well hidden amid undergrowth, or under a large furze bush. It is one of the most difficult nests to locate, and the birds enter and leave the surrounding cover some distance from the nest rather than run the risk of betraying its whereabouts.

I once waited for an hour in the hope of seeing a male stonechat deposit, on his partly finished nest, a grass stem which he was carrying, but I waited in vain. For a time the bird flitted here and there, still holding the grass stem in his beak; then he would drop his building material, and in his metallic " u-tec, u-tec " call-notes scold me severely for my intrusion, before again picking up the stalk.

It was I who gave in, and before I had gone a dozen yards the stonechat had disappeared in the hedgerow, probably feeling proud of himself for having outdone my patience. It is easier to locate the stonechat's nest when there are young to be fed, for the noisy chorus of the little ones as they welcome their parents with food often provides a clue to their exact whereabouts.

The five or six pale, greenish-blue eggs are spotted and blotched with reddish - brown at the larger end. Two broods are raised in a season.

The whinchat haunts a similar type of country to the stonechat, but differs from that bird in that it is a summer visitor to this country, arriving in April. The two birds outwardly resemble one another somewhat, although the differences are sufficient to distinguish easily one from the other. The male birds especially may be easily identified, the whinchat having a conspicuous white eye-stripe whilst its breast does not nearly approach the brilliance of that of the stonechat.

The whinchat loves the gorse of the fields and heathlands, and once the birds have reached this country and paired, each wedded couple confine themselves to a certain portion of territory; outside that area they seldom stray, except on hurried excursions for food, whilst inside that area no other bird is welcome. Both the stonechats and the whinchats, once they have paired, live solitary lives—just the husband and his wife alone with their responsibilities and family affairs. I am fond of watching the chats going about their daily routine because of the serious-minded way they attend to their duties.

In their nesting habits they closely resemble the stonechat, except that the situation chosen is more often on the ground itself. The nest is just as difficult to discover, however, it being carefully concealed in herbage; it is more neatly made than the nest of the stonechat, but similar materials are used.

The four or five eggs are greenish-blue in ground colour, faintly spotted with reddish-brown, but the markings vary considerably; sometimes blotches and streaks are present, more especially on the larger end.

The greater and lesser whitethroats are birds of the warbler family which haunt fields and

143

commons. The greater whitethroat, generally known as the whitethroat, is, as its name implies, the larger of the two. Because of its fondness for nettle beds the bird is often termed the nettle-creeper. It is surprising how strongly these local names for birds and animals become established, and a few years ago I was surprised to find that, in a certain district, no one seemed ever to have heard of a whitethroat whilst the nettle-creeper was a familiar bird. In that same district the meadow pipit was known as the titlark, and when I tried to explain to an aged farmer that meadow pipit was the correct name for this bird he was thoroughly annoyed. " I have seen many more summers than you have, mister," was his retort, " and titlarks was here before I was and will be here after I'm gone—I ain't got no patience with these new-fangled names for birds and things."

For courtesy's sake I will withhold the name of that particular district, but in spite of the charming and sociable inhabitants it was a most amazing place for nicknames; even the neighbours called each other by pet names and responded to them.

The whitethroat is a migrant bird and reaches these shores about the middle of April. The bird soon announces its arrival by its jerky song, which although far from being musical, is a cheery chatter and characteristic of the liveliness of the singer. Sometimes the song is uttered from a patch of tangled bracken, a gorse bush, or from some wayside herbage; seldom does the whitethroat occupy a prominent perch when singing, but it does sometimes shoot up into the air singing the while.

The bird is generally distributed throughout Britain, but becomes less numerous in the extreme northern districts of Scotland. The whitethroat is a very determined songster, and even during the hottest hour of a summer's day continues to utter its energetic melody. It is a great lover of sunshine, and at midday in summer when, as most nature students have noticed, the majority of birds seek an hour's shade in the recesses of some tree or hedge, the whitethroat is actively alive in the full glare of the sunshine.

Indeed, its nest is often constructed where little shade protects it from the sun's scorching rays, and it is not unusual to see the sitting bird with beak wide open panting with the heat. Both sexes share the duties of incubation, and I have several times seen one or other of the parents perched on the side of the nest with wings outstretched to afford shade to the fledglings.

The whitethroat is a cheerful bird and by no means shy provided you remain a reasonable distance from its nest, but when an intruder

approaches too closely, the bird changes its behaviour and seems to lose all its original boldness
and determination. Instead, it skulks through the
bracken or bushes, uttering its little harsh scolds
and keeping well out of sight.

The whitethroat frequents almost any type of
country except woodland and marshes. Occasionally a nesting pair take up residence in the out-
skirts of a coppice, but seldom do the birds enter
the inner parts of wooded areas. It is also rare
to find them nesting in marshes, and only once
have I recorded a whitethroat's nest in a reed
bed.

Nettle beds are favourite nesting sites, but nests
in tangled herbage, brambles and in low-growing
gorse bushes are often found. It is seldom more
than two feet above ground, and is a neatly made
structure of roots, grass stems and finer grasses
with a lining of hair. From four to six eggs are
laid, brownish-yellow in colour, blotched and
spotted with brown and grey. The eggs hatch
in about thirteen days, and by the end of May
fledglings are not unusual. This is rather early
in the year for migrant birds to have families,
but of all our summer visitors the whitethroat
is the first to settle down to domestic affairs.

The vicinity of the nest is often betrayed by
the excited behaviour of whichever of the two
birds is off duty. Even so, the sitting mate

MALE STONECHAT WITH FOOD

continues to incubate closely even though an intruder is within arm's reach of her.

The devoted and hard-working parents rear their young quickly, and a second brood is sometimes raised in a season. Some writers, however, aver that the nests found in June and July are the result of first nests being destroyed and that only one brood is raised each year. It is within my own knowledge, however, that whitethroats are sometimes double-brooded. Another point in dispute among bird-lovers concerns the building of the nest, some folk saying that the male bird is solely responsible, while others state that the hen bird alone is the architect. I am able to say that neither opinion is right, for the birds share the duties of nest-building and incubation.

The lesser whitethroat is a slightly smaller bird than its near relative, and its white throat-patch is less pronounced. It is a greyer and more drab little bird than the greater whitethroat and is less widely distributed. Later years, however, show some signs of the bird extending its range. In England it is mainly confined to the southern and midland counties, but for some three or four years I have received authentic information of nests in Cornwall. As a rare visitor it occurs in Wales, Scotland and Ireland.

The lesser whitethroat is a more shy and retiring species than the greater whitethroat, but its nesting habits are practically the same, except that it occasionally provides its nest with a lining of hair. The eggs, from four to six, are yellowish-white, spotted and blotched with greys and browns.

It is a far less domineering bird than the commoner whitethroat, and instead of the fussy behaviour so marked in the latter species when one approaches its nesting territory, the lesser whitethroat conceals itself in the bushes, from which one may hear its occasional scolding notes.

INDEX

INDEX